Lean Six Sigma: Coach Me If You Can

The True Story of Practical Lean Six Sigma Coaching

Anne Ponton

ISBN: 1470162407
ISBN: 9781470162405

Contents

Preface

So many Black Belts and Master Black Belts, passionate about their own experience with Lean Six Sigma and eager to communicate their passion, end up pulling "Green- or Black-Belt-to-be" without any tangible result. Are you one of them? Have you been in a Lean Six Sigma training class, trying your best to make the methodology clear and pragmatic enough to switch on light bulbs yet convinced that half of the people in the room are only half-committed and will not even start a Green Belt journey, let alone get a certification? Or have you been attending a Lean Six Sigma training class hoping to learn methodologies, tips and tools, but discouraged after the first half-day from catching anything practical out of the time invested in the class? Why is that? What separates a successful Lean Six Sigma development journey from one that fails? What does success mean as it relates to coaching and mentoring future Lean Six Sigma experts? How can *you*, a successful Lean Six Sigma expert, nurture new blood and let your own passion and success infect someone else, who will, in turn, be as passionate and impactful as you are?

Lean Six Sigma: Coach Me if You Can aims at providing landmarks to make such a development journey insightful, transformational, and successful. The pages you are about to read highlight the traps along the journey that might compromise success and suggest some tips for walking around those traps.

This is not a novel to be read at the bed table. It is a *cookbook*, meant to be practical and insightful. Coach or mentor of Green and Black Belt-to-be, you will find numerous recipes to digest and use in your own sauce. Lean Six Sigma project manager or trainee embarking on one of your first Lean Six Sigma journeys, you will find some landmarks for self-guidance, helping you to become your own coach and find your way in the dense Lean Six Sigma jungle. Sponsor of a

Lean Six Sigma journey, manager of a future Lean Six Sigma expert, or curious reader keen to learn about the Lean Six Sigma mind-set, you will find a practical overview of what such a journey brings to your business and people. Yet, whoever you are, if you want to get the full benefit of this book I am begging you: Pause and think about what all of this means to you. How are you going to make it relevant and practical in your own kitchen?

Lean Six Sigma: Coach Me if You Can does not provide answers to your business challenges; it helps you to ask the right questions at the right time. Answering these questions by yourself will help you to reach your goals in your own environment, taking into consideration your own constraints. But it can only happen if *you* bring the answers. At the end of each paragraph, and whenever you feel the need, think about a few things you are going to do differently after reading this book and how transformational that will be for you and the people around you. Write down what you are going to change in your own world in the *"Your Notes"* section placed for this purpose at the end of the book; come back to your notes once in a while, until the behaviors you have recorded become naturally embedded in your day-to-day habits. And I promise, you *will* see the difference.

The story line follows the Lean Six Sigma journey, starting with its preparation and foundations, following its flow from Define to Control, and ending with a reflection on the learning and takeaway for the coach and the new Belt.

The behavioral transformation and soft skills expected from the future Lean Six Sigma experts along the course of their development are emphasized. Many books are already on the shelf about technical Lean Six Sigma tools, and most companies applying this methodology have their own in-house materials as well. Thus the technicalities of the Lean Six Sigma tools are secondary here. For each step of the journey, a few technical elements key to development will be highlighted (the *hardware*), but the mind-set and nontechnical tips that contribute to the difference between success and failure (the *software*) will be the focus of this book.

CHAPTER 1

Creating the Momentum for Success

*Positive Energy is the opposite of money:
the more you spend, the more you have,
and the more you communicate to others.*

How do you initiate and drive a Lean Six Sigma journey with enthusiasm and passion? What does "good" look like when delivering on a Lean Six Sigma journey while at the same time building a Lean Six Sigma expert? How do you prepare a well-balanced suitcase, taking into account the constraints of a given business environment? These are the questions we will begin with.

Positive Energy: The Fuel for Constructive Coaching

The energy of the mind is the essence of life.
—*Aristotle*

Few candidates for a Green or Black Belt journey start with a *fire in the belly* to become a Green or Black Belt. Some start because their managers ask them to do so; others start because it "looks good," or because they see it as a mandatory box to be ticked to have a successful leadership career. None of these motivations provide enough kinetic energy to overcome the challenges of a process-improvement journey. This is precisely where the coach or mentor comes in, with the heavy duty of gathering and spreading *Positive Energy* all along the way, from the beginning to the end of the journey.

As the coach, begin the journey with Positive Energy and optimism, and keep it up all along to feed the Belt and the stakeholders with enthusiasm and passion. You may visualize Positive Energy as a smile, a ray of sunlight, or a breath of fresh air. Give a smile: you will feel happier and see people smiling at you in return. Catch a ray of sunlight coming through the window: you will feel enlightened, and the entire room will look brighter. Take a deep breath of fresh air: you will feel soothed and will see people around you relaxing as well. You give, you get in return, and you get even more to share.

Positive Energy brings a good mood and happiness, making people proactive, constructive, and energetic to walk the Lean Six Sigma journey as though they were cheerfully singing. But that is not all. Research – conducted by famous neuroscientists all around the world, including in the University of Oxford, UK, or in the University of Stanford, USA, to quote only two among dozens – shows that when people work with a positive mind-set, productivity, creativity, and engagement improve. People perform at their best when they visualize their contribution to a positive goal. Training your brain to be positive is like training your muscles when working out: it helps you to improve and perform. Would you believe that a good physical training degrades performance? Of course not! Similarly, everyone performs better with a positive brain when facing a challenge.

From the beginning, and all along the Lean Six Sigma journey, the coach is the one responsible for filling up the tank with Positive Energy. Positive Energy is a driving force, a catalyst, creating inspiration and enthusiasm, bringing motivation to the learner to overcome the challenges faced along the road, eventually raising the learning curve up to the sky and preventing progress from flattening.

Success is not final; failure is not fatal: it is the courage to continue that counts.—Winston Churchill As a coach and mentor, see yourself as the *Positive Energy PIT STOP,* where Green or Black Belts-to-be will fill their tanks. You are accountable for alimenting and renewing the driving force, providing the courage to continue the journey to the end of the road.

What does being a Positive Energy PIT STOP practically mean for you, as the coach or mentor? First of all, it means that if you happen to run out of Positive Energy, the Green or Black Belt-to-be will feel it and will likely end up demotivated, less productive, less creative, and less engaged. Positive Energy is the opposite of money: the more you spend, the more you have—and the more you communicate to others and spread positive thinking, motivation, enthusiasm, and passion around you. Do not be shy: spend it! You will never run out of it; instead, you will get even more for yourself and for others! Meet with Green or Black Belts-to-be frequently, and sow the seeds of Positive Energy so they can see the adventure as an exhilarating roller coaster, rather than a boring, steep, and winding track.

Being a Positive Energy PIT STOP also means that you have to be able to read the gauge of the Green or Black Belt-to-be: How much Positive Energy do you need to provide? When? Which type of "fuel" is missing? There is no black-or-white answer to these questions, which means that your emotional intelligence is a key factor for success in the journey. You, as the coach or mentor, have to feel what the learner needs from you, be it technical or *human.* And for sure, you will need to provide both technical and human energy to successfully reach the finish line: technical energy to raise the technical Lean Six Sigma learning curve up to the sky; human energy to create and maintain the momentum, feeding the enthusiasm and accelerating the progress.

How to Measure Success?

*Always bear in mind that your own resolution to succeed
is more important than any other*
—Abraham Lincoln

What does success mean? What are the Critical-To-Quality criteria in building a Lean Six Sigma expert? As a Master Black Belt myself, I do not believe we could start the journey without first defining our objectives and answering those questions. So let's pause here and think about our key success factors in developing Lean Six Sigma experts.

Only a life lived for others is a life worthwhile. —Albert Einstein Think about those words from the perspective of a Lean Six Sigma mentor. Do they mean that the development of the people matters beyond anything else? What should be expected from a recognized Lean Six Sigma expert?

Mastering the technical and analytical Lean Six Sigma tools

Obviously, the Green or Black Belt-to-be is expected to learn and master the technical aspects of the DMAEC / DMAIC methodology (Define, Measure, Analyze, Engineer / Improve, Control) and to identify the need to apply the tools practically in his/her own environment. This means that the learner must be able to step back and understand the contents and outputs of each tool, beyond the theory and beyond the specific case study being used for development. As an outcome of such maturity gained when learning the technical tools, the learner should be able to anticipate the benefits the Lean Six Sigma tools can bring outside of a specific project and how those tools can be used at any time to answer a business need. In summary, mastering the Lean Six Sigma toolbox means to *catch the Lean Six Sigma technicalities and mind-set.*

Solving problems

Coaching aims at helping people meet their full potential: not making their goals but helping people to reach them. The coach is not the one to give the solution; the coach asks the right questions and opens horizons, switches on the light bulb, and changes the vision, which ultimately provokes learners to find the answers themselves. To this point, have you noticed we commonly speak about "trainees" but never "coachees"? This is because "being coached" should not be a passive listening process led by the coach but rather an active journey, merely guided by the coach.

So how do you guide without leading? How do you position the learner in an active driver's seat—as opposed to a passive, subordinate passenger's seat? By asking the right questions. Asking questions instead of providing answers forces learners to self-reflect and guides them toward building the thought process to come up with an answer themselves. By building in this reflex to ask questions when facing a roadblock, you are tremendously contributing to the development of their *problem solving* skills and *positive thinking*. Learning to resolve problems or walk around them by opening up a different mind-set and creating a forward motion instead of seeing a closed door when challenges arise is extremely helpful. As a consequence, the future Lean Six Sigma expert learns to identify and define problems, self-reflect on how to confront them, and turn them into opportunities and solutions.

This tactic also helps the coach to be more understanding and less directive, allowing a strong human relationship of credibility and trust to develop between the coach and the learner. Furthermore, the coach does not have *the* right answer to everything and does not speak God's word but is a human being, as the learner is, who needs self-reflection and understanding of the context. Letting the learner answer the questions then helps both the coach and the learner to step-back and gain some insight in a field most likely better mastered by the subject matter experts accompanying the project team in the journey to define, understand and resolve the problems to be fixed as an outcome of the project.

Leading change and managing projects

Basic project management skills are obviously mandatory in leading a successful Lean Six Sigma initiative. I am not referring here to any advanced project management techniques, but to the basics of being able to identify and mitigate project risks, manage key stakeholders, and build and track a simple project plan.

Yet *change management* is an important topic to be taken away from such a journey: Lean Six Sigma projects target *improvement*; improvement requires change, and making the change happen requires skills. Green or Black Belts-to-be must learn and build those skills before being recognized as experts. At the end of the journey, they must have proven their ability to *sell* change and motivate others, with or without a direct reporting line. This requires that they build leadership skills and a certain ability to attract credibility and trust.

Presenting and communicating with impact

Presentation and communication skills must be part of the suitcase of a good Lean Six Sigma expert. As such, the learner must end the journey able to articulate a good message and presentation, telling a meaningful and impactful "story" to any level of management (vertically and horizontally), stepping back from the technical tools and speaking the language of the business. Only after those skills are brought to the next level does the Belt become able to negotiate and influence decision making with tact and professionalism.

Education is the most powerful tool that can be used to change the world. —Nelson Mandela Developing influential change leaders with strong problem solving and communication skills is the foundation of a successful and sustainable organization in a mobile and dynamic environment in constant appetite for what is going to come next.

Making an impact to the business

Yet let's not be so naïve to believe that, in a modern corporate environment, managers can afford to spend their resources purely to develop people. This is why the Lean Six Sigma development journey is so powerful: people are trained and coached on case studies while delivering real impact and tangible benefits to their business during the course of their learning journey. They learn to drive in a real car, on a real road! And the greater the real-life benefits a Lean Six Sigma journey targets, the greater the interest that will be raised and the more that is going to be expected from the Green or Black Belt...ending in a self-perpetuating circle where the Belt-to-be has to learn more to meet those expectations.

How big or how small the business need is does not matter and is surely to be assessed in each individual context, but if there is no case to justify the need for a Lean Six Sigma expert, the journey is likely to be dull and disappointing to the learner.

So in a nutshell, the key success factors of the journey depend on both customers: the learner and the management investing in the development of the person. Learners expect to be transformed by their journey and to be able to replicate the best practices and leverage the skills built along the way; managers expect to get direct benefits for the business with a return on investment as high as possible, with the lessons learned to be straightforwardly reused in another upcoming business challenge. Both customers have to be satisfied. Are those expectations synergistic or antagonistic? Think about it, and answer for yourself.

We will analyze together after the development journey how meeting such customers expectations practically translates into catching hard and soft Lean Six Sigma skills.

A Journey Bound to Succeed

Success is a science; if you have the conditions, you get the result.
—*Oscar Wilde*

Once you are well aware of what is expected from the journey, the next question is how to get there.

What if coaches could rely on a short list of the key ingredients they need to gather at the beginning of the journey, providing a 95 percent confidence that the journey will be a success? Without pretending that anybody could possess a sample of Lean Six Sigma initiatives large enough to represent with 95 percent confidence the gigantic diversity and plurality of Lean Six Sigma initiatives, let's reflect on the differences between Lean Six Sigma journeys that succeed and those that fail.

At this point, I would like to highlight four cornerstones.

Buy-ins and commitments: witnessing the contribution to a broader strategic objective

As a direct outcome of the list of key success factors from both customers—learner and management—the first elements to bring in are commitments (yes, plural): commitment that the learner will have enough time all along the journey as well as enough motivation to *take* the time required for a hands-on development methodology; and commitment from the management to support the learner in the difficult moments and help the learner drive the change.

Learning and building the robust skills listed in the previous paragraph requires *time*. *Time* is not something one finds; it is something one takes. The lack of top and middle management patience and buy-in are among the most frequent root causes for Lean Six Sigma initiative failure, as it results in the Green or Black Belt-to-be not being empowered to *take the time* required to make the journey a success.

Furthermore, the commitment of the management to dedicate time and allocate resources to a Lean Six Sigma initiative, whatever big or small, is strong evidence that the initiative contributes to delivering a broader strategy. People only bother with things that matter, and if nobody bothers, the project is not likely to matter much. As soon as a more important challenge pops up, the resources are going to be reallocated, leaving the Lean Six Sigma journey aside before it truly delivers benefits to the business. Why spend time and effort on something that does not matter? Look at what interests decisions makers and senior management; concentrate on what matters.

The role of the coach is not only to ensure support is present and strong from the beginning but also to inject the required flow of Positive Energy along the journey if the level of patience and buy-in drops. On top of continuously supporting the Belt-to-be to deliver, implementing these techniques is a way to stress-test the adherence and relevance of the initiative to a broader strategic objective, guaranteeing the fact that you are neither wasting your time as a coach, nor wasting the time of the Belt and other stakeholders involved in the project.

A business problem that must be fixed, without a known solution

Still one of the basic ingredients of a successful journey is the quality of the underlying product: the *raw material*. A Lean Six Sigma project starts with a *problem* for which the solution is *not* known. If you know the solution, go and implement it! Do not spend months of frustration in Define, Measure, and Analyze only to end up doing what you already knew—reinventing the wheel, as it were. A Lean Six Sigma project providing a positive experience to the learner starts with a business challenge for which the business owner (i.e., the management) is eager to see a practical answer yet has no or very little clue of what this answer should be at the start. You may call it a problem statement, opportunity statement, or whatever else; in essence, it means to answer a few questions: *What is the problem? Why is it a problem? How do I know it really is a problem? Do I know a simple, realistic solution to resolve the problem?*

Without the need to answer such questions from a business perspective, or without meaningful answers to those questions (in the language of the business), the Lean Six Sigma initiative is likely to mean using some tools for the sake of using the tools—rather than for the answers they bring. That scenario will result in a bad experience for the learner, who does not believe the tools have any added value beyond common sense. As a result, that learner will not build technical skills strong enough to replicate the usage of the tools in another context, and that results in a bad experience for the management, who comes up with the impression that time is spent in administrative steps aimed at ticking boxes in a checklist of tools to learn rather than delivering valuable analysis, which eventually leads to a loss of patience and buy-in.

A broken, inefficient, or risky process in the eyes of the customers

This may be obvious to many Lean Six Sigma experts, but the Lean Six Sigma tools are relevant in analyzing *processes* and help to make data-driven decisions to *improve* the initial situation. So, as a starting point, an important foundation is the underlying process, the *transformation path* of the input into the output. For the Lean Six Sigma approach to be meaningful, relevant, and beneficial, the *problem* that needs to be resolved should come from the *process*. And the management, supportive of the initiative, should have the means to act as a decision maker in changing the *process*.

Adapted and relevant objectives, with significant and meaningful expectations to deliver value to the customers

A common and too often seen pitfall in Lean Six Sigma initiatives is using this methodology because it is on shelf, rather than because it suits a business need and objective to add value to the customers and deliver material impact to the business. I can think of four types of objectives that fit well into Lean Six Sigma initiatives.

The first type aims at *improving quality*. Poor quality is measured by a certain number of defects coming out of a process. The initiative should aim at reducing those defects, resulting in a reduction of the Cost of Poor Quality (COPQ). For example, poor quality out of any reporting process could be materialized by the number of errors in the reports after the first production; the COPQ would then be the time required to review the reports and correct the errors made at the first trial. A Lean Six Sigma project could here aim at reducing the number of errors at the first trial; as a consequence, less time would be spent on correcting the reports, hence the COPQ would reduce.

The second type of objective aims at *reducing process risk*. This differs from improving quality in that defects have not yet been materialized; hence, poor quality cannot yet be measured in number of defects. However, a Lean Six Sigma initiative can bring value here by preventing defects and severe issues from happening in the first place, resulting in stabilizing the process and making it safe, in control. The Risk Priority Number (RPN) from the Failure Modes Effects

Analysis (FMEA) can be used as a metric. We will explore this concept further in Chapter Three. You may also refer to the definition of an FMEA in the glossary for a brief introduction.

The third type aims at *reducing cycle time*. The time taken between the start and end of the process must be reduced. This includes processing and waiting times, inventories, and queues. For example, the objective of a Lean Six Sigma project could be to reduce the overall time required for clients to open a bank account: the process starts when the clients initiate the account opening request and ends when the account is open and usable by the clients, or when the request is rejected by the bank. The total cycle time is made of the time to fill in and process the application, the time when the application potentially waits for a bank officer to be available, the time when the client comes to the bank branch and potentially queues until a bank clerk is available... every single second between the initiation of the request and its completion.

The fourth type of objective aims at *increasing process capacity*—in other words, doing more with less. The metrics are a combination of processing time (hours worked, excluding waiting and idle time) and volumes of process inputs. Process inputs can be, for example, the number of clients' calls coming into a call center in a day, or the number of payments and cash transfers to be executed in a financial institution in one month. The process capacity is represented by the working time to deal with the entire volume of process inputs. Hence, the process capacity can be increased by both reducing the number of inputs coming into the manual process (for example reducing the number of clients calling to raise complaints), and / or reducing the time spent on processing each input (for example reducing the workload necessary to perform a payment or a cash transfer).

While *quality* and *cycle time* types of initiatives tend to, as a consequence, target to improve customer satisfaction (external), *risk* and *capacity* projects tend to be driven by the need to improve process owner performance and optimize processing costs (internal).

Any Lean Six Sigma initiative can, of course, be a combination of several of those four, but to make it a meaningful and relevant, yet realistic and achievable Lean Six Sigma effort, the focus should be kept to improving one or two of them while the others should at least be maintained.

The Golden Triangle of Lean Six Sigma projects

Time, Capacity

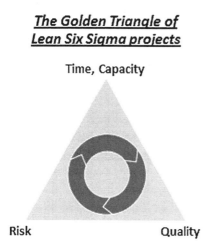

Risk   Quality

Eventually all four objectives begin to work synergistically: improving quality results in reducing the risk for the process to fail, which results in spending less time correcting errors, which results in less pressure, fewer defects, and better quality. Where to start is a matter of priority. Just be sure to start somewhere where it matters.

Also bear in mind that patience and perseverance are required to resolve several challenges in parallel: targeting to resolve the hunger of the world is likely to result in a never-ending effort, filled with frustration and discouragements. As an illustration, would you be more likely to succeed in the mission to feed all the starving African children, or in the mission to cook soups and bread to the homeless people in your neighborhood? I am sure the latter looks a lot more manageable to you as it does to me. Yet, little by little, if we could imagine finding patient and perseverant volunteers in all corners of the world to cook soups and bread following your recipe and action plan, the hunger of the world would drastically reduce, even if it is never going to totally disappear. But if you start with the intention to feed all starving people, everywhere in the world, the risk is simply to achieve nothing at all. Rather start by preparing simple and practical recipes, feed your neighborhood, measure tangible benefits, and expand little by little to achieve bigger goals.

In summary, stay grounded when defining your goals, but do challenge yourself to achieve bigger goals whilst not destroying what works already well. In practice, define two categories of goals whilst remaining realistic, optimistic, and thrilling on challenges: improvement goals (how much of the problem is expected to be resolved), as well as "watchdog" goals (what should not be degraded whilst resolving the problem). With such a bi-dimensional mission, you are set to efficiently but pragmatically contribute to resolve the biggest problems in your company, little by little, whilst maintaining what works well and leveraging on the enthusiasm created by incremental successes to raise up the Positive Energy to confront the next and biggest challenges.

I bet that if all Lean Six Sigma development journeys could start with these four cornerstones—(1) buy-ins and commitments, (2) a business problem important to resolve, without the solution being known from the start, (3) a broken, inefficient, or risky process (in the eyes of the customers) responsible for the problem, and (4) an objective to either improve quality, reduce process risk, reduce cycle time, or increase process capacity—the success rate would be greater than 95 percent. These four fundamentals might be obvious to you, and I am happy if they are, but I truly believe that due diligence in exploring them before rushing into the start of your journey will make all the difference between success and failure.

The 4 Cornerstones of "good" Lean Six Sigma development journeys

Buy-ins and Commitments witnessing the contribution to a broader strategic objective	A business *Problem* important to be fixed, without a known solution
A "good" Lean Six Sigma development opportunity	
A broken, risky or inefficient process in the eyes of the customers	Adapted objectives with significant and meaningful expectations: improve quality, reduce risk, reduce cycle time, increase capacity

"Success is getting what you want. Happiness is wanting what you get," said Dale Carnegie, an American writer famous for his self-improvement studies. Know what you and your customers want; be transparent and honest with yourself on these checkpoints, and you are likely to reach a happy end by proactively transforming what you want into what you get. Do not begin the journey if you are not 95 percent confident it is going to be a success, especially if the journey involves you, the

coach, and a learner likely to live his first Lean Six Sigma experience! Be sure the memory of the honeymoon sets the scene for an optimistic and happy life thereafter.

It is now time to pause and think about what all this means to you. The following self-reflective questionnaire can help you to find out the following:

- How do you visualize *Positive Energy* in your own environment?
- How could you create *Positive Energy* around you?
- Are you ready to sow the seeds of *Positive Energy* necessary to feed the journey?
- Who are your customers, and what does "good" look like to them?
- What practical actions would work to spend and spread *Positive Energy* among your stakeholders?
- Do you have an underlying problem justifying the need for a Lean Six Sigma journey?
- Does everyone agree the problem is a real pain that *must* be fixed?
- Why do some stakeholders think the problem is not worth fixing?

Do not lie; Be true to yourself and to your customers.

CHAPTER TWO

The Foundations of a Fulfilling and Successful Journey

*A successful man is one who can lay a firm foundation
with the bricks others have thrown at him.*
—*David Brinkley*

Preparing the scaffold before the journey and maintaining its solidity all along makes a great difference between success and failure when building a Lean Six Sigma expert. However, let's not forget that *"Well done is better than well said,"* to follow Benjamin Franklin's advice. If the role of the coach is surely not to drive the Lean Six Sigma initiative itself, he/she can be of tremendous value by preparing the road, structuring the journey, and materializing the progress—not just with words and passions but with practical actions that will *build* the expertise and mind-set step by step upon strong roots. This chapter provides a few models best seen as the bricks coaches, trainers, trainees and managers can use to build robust foundations.

Structuring the Journey

It is better to travel well than to arrive.
—*Dalai Lama*

The "TAKT time" (German word for "stroke") or pace of the initiative and its deliveries is a key component of keeping the momentum created at the beginning of the journey and maintaining the level of Positive Energy injected into it. A project is more likely to succeed if it has a short and dynamic life cycle, with quick and responsive deliverables. This is especially true in a corporate organization constantly threatened by environmental changes and pressurized by restrictions, where managers are only looking for benefits concretely and immediately contributing to increased value to the customers and activities of their organization.

Therefore, constantly keeping in mind the idea of short-term and fast-paced deliverables, coach and Belt-to-be should meet regularly and frequently—weekly is a frequency that has proved successful. Each coaching session should be structured and have a concrete and materialized outcome on which the learner can rely to build the next step of the journey. In other words, these coaching sessions represent *Positive Energy PIT STOP*. After each session, the tank of Positive Energy must be full enough to reach the next PIT STOP, i.e., the next coaching session.

The T-GROW model, structuring a coaching session in five steps – set the *topic*; define the *goals*; capture the *reality* of the achievements; explore the possible *options* to achieve the goals; assess the true *will* to achieve the goals – has proven successful in structuring coach/Belt interactions, and this book does not aim at reinventing current models or theories. So, let's concentrate on the practical steps and outcomes of a productive coach/Green or Black Belt-to-be discussion from a coach's perspective.

As mentioned in the first chapter, an effective coaching session that delivers constructive springboard results should be seen as a PIT STOP: Positively open, Interrogate, Test, Structure, Traps, Organize, Prepare. Let's go through each of these steps one by one.

Start with a cheerful *positive opening,* questioning the Belts-to-be on what they want to speak about. Asking them the topics to be covered forces them to recall the context and review what they are doing and why. It also helps you, the coach, to remember at which stage the journey was left. By answering this question, learners set the objectives for the day and become the driver of what needs to be done next.

Next, *interrogate* and let Green or Black Belts-to-be explain what they have completed since your last session. Let me emphasize here that I am talking about genuine, deep questioning, not just a list of pre-defined questions asked one after the other without any connection but two, three, or more levels of questioning. You might prepare the first level of questions (some guiding examples are listed for each topic in Chapter Three). But then, you will have to actively listen to the answer, truly understand it in the language of the business's context, and dig further by asking the next questions according to the answer provided to the first level of questions. Asking several levels of questions, one question built upon the answer to the previous one, will force both Belts-to-be and you to go deeper and further in analyzing the subject and defining the appropriate next steps. *"So what?"* should always be somewhere in the back of your mind until you clearly hear from the Belt-to-be the link with the ultimate objectives of the journey. Furthermore, in addition to informing you, the coach, of the progress, letting Belts-to-be provide the answers forces them to explain what they have done—and I do not think there is a better way to learn than by teaching or explaining to someone else. Give this opportunity to Belts-to-be. They know that you already know and they are proud to tell you all the good work they have done, and to show you they know it as well. It also helps to develop their presentation and communication skills—one of our key success factors in developing process improvements experts—especially if the coach emphasizes the need for providing simple, clear, concise explanations.

The answers provided by Belts-to-be should be a means for you, the coach, to *test* the strength of the Lean Six Sigma technical knowledge. Not only does it help learners to visualize the progress and the path, but it also forces them to review the tools and synthesize their learning: What was learned from each tool? What difference was made in the definition, understanding, and resolution of the problem thanks to a rigorous application of the method? If need be, the coach might recall the technical aspects learned during the theoretical training: the training, usually attended prior to the project, will have laid the foundations of the technical knowledge; yet some elements of the Lean Six Sigma methodology might have been missed or forgotten. Each coaching session is a good opportunity to strengthen the technical skills, so do not miss that chance if you think such reminders are necessary.

The outcomes and conclusions of the above *interrogate* and *test* steps should help Belts-to-be naturally transition to the next step, with enthusiasm thanks to the *positive opening*. *Structure* the next step by actively questioning Belts-to-be on lessons learned from the tasks completed and asking them what needs to be studied next (in the immediate term) to achieve the next project milestone (short to medium term).

Then, look at potential *traps:* reflect on the difficulties and roadblocks to be expected, and challenge Green or Black Belts-to-be on how those risks are going to be mitigated. This may require deploying additional Lean Six Sigma tools or digging further and deeper into some tools already used. It may also highlight the need to develop specific soft skills or to reach out to some stakeholders for support or arbitration (sponsor, process owner or else), but ultimately, the answers should come from the learner, deeply guided by several levels of self-reflective questions from the coach.

Finish with a short summary of the next steps, helping Belts-to-be to conceptualize, visualize, and interiorize the learning, empowering them to *organize* themselves in preparation for what they will do next.

Prepare them to concentrate on what is critical to achieve to safely take the next turns and continue moving forward, as opposed to what is "nice to have." Nothing could be worse than finishing with a dead end. Remember that, as the coach will not do the work, Belts-to-be should have the means to do it. Ensure they practically know what to do next, have all they need from you, the coach, to do it, and have enough Positive Energy to overcome the challenges that might arise before the next Positive Energy PIT STOP.

The PIT STOP checklist:
A proactive coaching session model

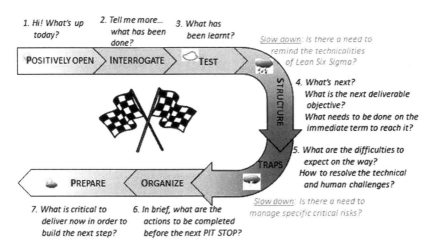

Systematically following those steps is likely to ensure the productive, proactive, and fruitful working coaching sessions necessary to successfully answer the business need. It will also tremendously help to keep a well-paced momentum of visual and material immediate-term to short-term deliverables, eventually building little by little the ultimate longer-term deliverable. An immediate-term deliverable might simply be to setup a meeting with the process owner to make him aware of a specific risk, or it might be to send an e-mail to teammates to ask their own vision of a specific challenge; a short-term deliverable might consist in organizing a meeting with a large group in advance, or preparing a document to be signed-off within a week or two. Such deliverables can really be anything that the Belt-to-be can visualize as an action step with a deliverable within a couple of weeks. Thus, progressing through each stage is an incremental and safe way to ensure the initiative is properly completed, meeting management expectations within time and budget.

Let me illustrate here the importance of small incremental steps in setting you and the Belt-to-be up for success in your Lean Six Sigma "marathon". Imagine you are given the objective to build a 10 storey-shopping mall. It looks like a huge task that will take years. Indeed, building a large shopping mall takes years. So where are you going to start? With the design on paper I guess. Followed by laying the foundations. And building up the first storey, the second, the third... and storey after storey up to the tenth, right? If you try to start from the tenth storey, you will not doubt the project is never going to succeed. So, as you want to succeed, you will obviously start with the design, the foundations and the first storey. Moreover, if you cleverly plan the construction of each storey, you might even start renting the shops on the first storeys before the tenth is fully completed, thus receiving incremental returns even before the completion of the project. Does it sound obvious when building a shopping mall? If yes, why should it be different when building or improving a process? The PIT-STOP checklist is a practical tool to apply to your Lean Six Sigma journey the "design first, then foundations, then storey after storey" principle.

Furthermore, such an incremental and safe progress contributes to build, little by little, the skills a Lean Six Sigma expert is expected to develop along the journey: *problem solving* skills as the coach asks questions and lets learners answer; *technical Lean Six Sigma expertise* by having learners explaining how they used the tools and which tools they will use for the next step; *project management and change leadership* skills by analyzing the risks and stakeholders' profiles and defining short-term objectives that will lead to meeting deadlines and managing customers' expectations; and *presentation and communication* skills by forcing learners to concisely explain what they have achieved.

Yet, to guarantee that each step of the journey is built one upon the other, the outcome of these coaching sessions should be materialized in a written record, helping the learner to stand on concrete bricks when lost in the journey. Let' study in the following section what such materialization means, and how to achieve the wanted objective to build each step of the journey upon the previous one.

Building the Expertise Step by Step

Action is the foundational key to all success
—Pablo Picasso

Along a Lean Six Sigma journey, enthusiasm for Green or Black Belts-to-be to overcome the challenges blocking the road can sometimes be like a dog crossing a highway: uncertain, challenged, and unsafe. Indeed, challenges, sometimes even roadblocks, are for sure going to come along the road. No Lean Six Sigma journey delivering real concrete benefits is following an easy and smooth path. So it is critical for the Belt-to-be to visualize the progress made and to move in only one direction: forward. While an athlete progresses "two steps forward, one step backward" to remain in good physical and mental health, Green or Black Belts-to-be should only be making progress and moving forward. This way, they will remain motivated and enthusiastic about their experiences, giving them the courage and energy to continue.

Yet the forward motion might not be practical and obvious at the end of a coaching session, as such meetings are likely to revolve around back-and-forth questions and answers rather than follow a clear, transparent structure.

An excellent method—that I promise has proven be of tremendous value for both coach and Belt-to-be—for materializing these steps with actions and keep forward momentum is for the coach to send a written summary after each coaching session, reminding Belts-to-be of the few actions to be completed within the week, before the next Positive Energy PIT STOP (it should be weekly, if you have followed me on the road so far): just a short, simple e-mail making the forward motion visual, concrete, and actionable.

Start the summary with a few words encouraging Green or Black Belts-to-be regarding their progress made since the previous session. Such encouragement makes them proud of having accomplished something on their own between two Positive Energy PIT STOP without the coach and eager to continue on their own. If no tangible progress has been made, still start with a positive message, injecting a flow of Positive Energy, and quickly but clearly emphasize the need to move to the next chapter. And if nothing at all has been accomplished, you may forward the previous summary, highlighting that the next steps remain the same. This emphasizes the lack of progress, and realizing nothing has been achieved usually provides an unconscious boost and sense of urgency to quickly move away from immobility. Yet find a positive message to encourage the Belt-to-be to move forward. An example of a simple yet realistic positive note could be: "You have done very well so far, let's not waste the efforts you have deployed to come up with such great work".

Then, list the next steps agreed upon at the end of the coaching session: the three or four actions to be completed in the week before the next Positive Energy PIT STOP. These actions must be achievable in the week and practical, without any specific challenge that the Belt-to-be could not overcome without the coach. Word them with *positive actions*: use "do" but avoid "don't." The brain ignores the "don'ts." Actions inject *Positive Energy* and constructive forward motion toward a positive goal; negations trigger resistance and backward motion. To convince you of this fact, let me ask you one thing: Don't think about a pink elephant. What do you picture in your mind? I bet you cannot help but see this silly, smiley pink elephant. Furthermore, if I had not spoken about a pink elephant, you would never have thought about it. Well, the same phenomenon happens in the minds of Belts-to-be if you ask them *not* to do something rather than encouraging them to do something. Be positive and the Belt-to-be will naturally interiorize the next steps while becoming eager to move forward.

Finally, end the summary with a positive encouragement, communicating again Positive Energy to the Green or Black Belts-to-be, and nailing down the fact that they are eager to move to the next step. Conclude with opening the possibility to reach out to you at any time if they face a roadblock and do not know what to do on their own. The ultimate impression should be anything that *opens* the universe of the Belts-to-be to the next achievement and prevents them from stopping the journey like absorbed in a black hole.

Writing and sending this summary will take you, the coach, five to ten minutes at the most, and, I guarantee, it will make an amazing difference.

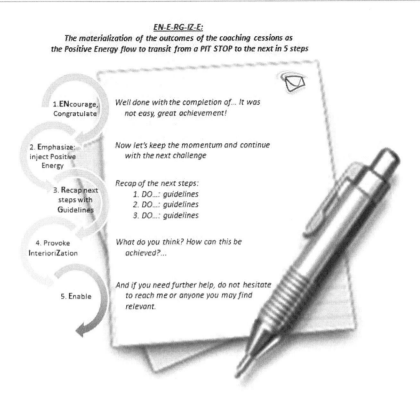

EN-E-RG-IZ-E:
The materialization of the outcomes of the coaching cessions as
the Positive Energy flow to transit from a PIT STOP to the next in 5 steps

1.ENcourage, Congratulate — Well done with the completion of... It was not easy, great achievement!

2. Emphasize; inject Positive Energy — Now let's keep the momentum and continue with the next challenge

3. Recap next steps with Guidelines — Recap of the next steps:
1. DO...: guidelines
2. DO...: guidelines
3. DO...: guidelines

4. Provoke InterioriZation — What do you think? How can this be achieved?...

5. Enable — And if you need further help, do not hesitate to reach me or anyone you may find relevant.

Such a written summary is beneficial for you, the coach, in that it first of all shows Green or Black Belts-to-be that you care about them, as you took the time to do it. It helps you to build this relationship of credibility and trust with your mentees, encouraging them to follow your advice rather than challenging them. Rigor and due diligence in this exercise will make you the person Belts-to-be do not want to disappoint, obviously resulting in raising the standard of the deliverables: They will work better and faster to show they are as committed as you are.

Such an encouraging summary is also tremendously valuable in many aspects for Belts-to-be. First, it provides *short-term*, achievable, and pragmatic objectives: something like a visual to-do list on the corner of a desk. Then, it represents a landmark: at any time, Belts-to-be can refer to it and visualize the motion and the flow—the Positive Energy—without having to recall what had been discussed and decided in their last Positive Energy PIT STOP. In addition, this practice avoids rework by materializing and engraving the progress. Finally, it leaves a written record for Belts-to-be to refer to in the long term, hence straightforwardly enabling the replication of the learning and best practices beyond a single, specific Lean Six Sigma project.

I promise, if you systematically write and send this summary, you will see the results. Not only will the Lean Six Sigma journey progress, and only progress, but you will also see commitment, credibility, and trust being established between you, the coach, and Belts-to-be, guaranteeing the Lean Six Sigma mind-set is robustly caught over time, one step forward after one step forward, one brick upon another. It is nothing but a win-win exercise.

Getting Set to Catch the Lean Six Sigma Mind-Set

Culture is what remains when one has forgotten everything.
—*Edouard Herriot*

What do I consider the Lean Six Sigma mind-set? What characterizes the thought process of a Lean Six Sigma expert compared to another change leader? What is the one thing the Lean Six Sigma expert must grasp from the start of the journey, laying the foundations of the inherited Lean Six Sigma mind-set and culture?

In essence, DMAEC / DMAIC is made up of five phases—Define, Measure, Analyze, Engineer / Improve, Control—but I see the thought process articulated around three key pillars:

1) *Define the problem.*
2) *Understand the problem.*
3) *Resolve the problem.*

Laying the foundations of the Lean Six Sigma mindset:
the 3-PILLAR actionable

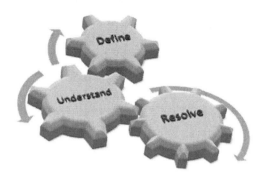

The first pillar, *define the problem,* refers to the Define phase, naturally setting as a prerequisite that a Lean Six Sigma initiative begins with a problem or a business challenge. The materialization of a clear definition of the problem is a list of key success factors (we will call them Critical-To-Quality, or CTQs in the next chapter): the three, four, or five specific, measurable objectives that have to be achieved, without which the initiative cannot be considered successful. Pillar One ends with a definition of the expected end state, setting up the project team to start with the end in mind.

The second pillar, *understand the problem*, is what the Measure and Analyze phases are made for. Plenty of tools are available to build a good understanding of the problem, and we will zoom into the list in the next chapter, but in brief, the problem can be considered understood once its *root causes* have been listed. Therefore, the objective of this second pillar is to *transform* a *business challenge*, by nature a complex, agglomerated problem, into a list of discrete and simply articulated problems called the root causes. Pillar Two ends with the list of key but simply articulated issues to be resolved and an assessment of the impact of each individual issue on the overall gap between the initial situation and the expected end clearly stated at the end of Pillar One.

The third pillar, *Resolve the problem,* aims at finding *solutions to the root causes* discovered in the second pillar, which eventually results in resolving for good the problem stated in the first pillar. The transformation of the second pillar helps to identify the easiest things to resolve in order to truly resolve the *business challenge* coming out of the first pillar on a long-term basis. Pillar Three ends once the expected end state has been reached and is proven to be stable over time.

You might think this three-pillar view is over-simplistic, and I am again happy if you do because to me, catching the Lean Six Sigma mind-set means developing the ability to *transform people and processes* by providing simple and robust foundations, laying the framework for growth beyond the journey.

Transforming *processes* is the fundamental objective of a Lean Six Sigma initiative. Pillar One: starting from a complex business challenge; Pillar Two: transforming it into a few simply articulated problems; and finally, Pillar Three: resolving these simple problems, which will result in the disappearance of the business challenge's symptoms.

Transforming the *people* is the primary mission of the coach; developing Lean Six Sigma experts starts with engraving this three-pillar mind-set in the learner's mind, which structures the data-driven, common sense thought process typical of Lean Six Sigma experts. As a consequence, such a simply structured approach to solve problems represents a powerful and robust approach, shaping people's minds and morphing any subject matter expert into an analytical mind able to resolve any problem going forward, whether that requires a full-scale project or not.

Let's illustrate this approach with a simple example that anyone can understand: Sally is sick today. She feels fever and stomach pain—the symptoms of the disease. She consults a doctor who has not captured the Lean Six Sigma mind-set. The doctor recalls treating another patient with the same symptoms with pain killers the previous week. He gives the same medicine. Sally feels better in the evening as the fever seems to drop slowly, but is sick again the next day.

Sally then consults another doctor, who has caught the Lean Six Sigma mind-set. He starts defining the problem: Sally has fever and stomach pain. He then works on understanding the problem and finds the underlying reason: Sally is contaminated by bacteria. Finally, the doctor finds the right antibiotic powerful enough to kill these specific bacteria (without any further medicine directly focused on fever and stomach pain). Sally gets better in a few days.

The first scenario, as simplistic and obvious as it is, happens every day in Lean Six Sigma initiatives when people are eager to jump to the end game and implement the solutions to patch the symptoms of their problems instead of truly resolving the problems. Because they cannot afford to spend the necessary time defining and understanding the problem, they never truly resolve it. When we attempt to save time by jumping to the end game, so much is lost in patches and quick "fixes" that eventually, the true root causes of the problems become hidden, making resolution increasingly complex, time-consuming, and costly.

As the builder of a successful Lean Six Sigma expert, start with the foundations: explain to the Green or Black Belt-to-be how powerful these three pillars (*Define, Understand, Resolve*) are in building robust and sustainable change. That is the very first step to get set in catching the Lean Six Sigma mind-set.

It is now, again, time to pause and think about what all this means to you with the help of the following self-reflective questions:

- Are you ready to pace the journey, meeting with Belts-to-be weekly?
- How are you going to practically deploy the PIT STOP checklist?
- Are you ready to take a few minutes after each PIT STOP session to EN-E-RG-IZ-E the learner, materializing these interactions and injecting your *Positive Energy* step by step?
- How are you going to ensure the Lean Six Sigma mind-set is truly caught, little by little all along the journey?

These bricks represent the scaffold of a strong and constructive Lean Six Sigma journey.

CHAPTER THREE

The Journey

Everyone thinks of changing the world, but no one thinks of changing himself.
—*Leo Tolstoy*

If you are still with me, I guess you have passed the initial questions and are now ready, eager to walk the talk…so let's go!

Preparation and Training

By failing to prepare, you are preparing to fail.
                                    —Benjamin Franklin

As the coach, you are responsible for the shape of the learning curve of Belts-to-be along the journey. It is your duty to let the journey start if and only if you honestly believe in its success from the beginning. The preparation phase should be a testing environment where you assess whether the criteria for success are strong enough. In essence, the motivation and eagerness of Green or Black Belts-to-be and of the business's sponsors and owners should be "stress tested" from the beginning, as should the necessity of deploying a Lean Six Sigma initiative.

Are the Belts-to-be keen to go onto such a journey because it "looks good", because they are asked to, or because they really *want* to do it? Do they know what to expect regarding the amount of time and effort committed into the journey? Have you, the coach, given the warnings, preparing the Belts-to-be to anticipate obstacles and making them aware of the necessity of investing time and effort and rolling up sleeves to overcome them? Though a Green Belt journey might be manageable without such awareness from the beginning, as the coach will be present and close all along to raise the Positive Energy level and reinforce the commitment, it is critical for a Black Belt, who will have to walk a much longer and more strenuous path. Without the burning desire to reach the end of the road, the time and energy invested at the start are likely to be wasted at the first or second roadblock.

Another of your missions as the coach is to validate the significance and relevance of the platform in which the Lean Six Sigma initiative is deployed. Is the business problem painful enough to be worth fixing? Does the opportunity matter enough for a business sponsor to invest resources in making some improvements? Will the business get some visible material benefits from the Lean Six Sigma initiative, justifying the investment? Will the business stakeholders be patient enough for the Belts-to-be to spend their time defining the problem and understanding it before finally resolving it? And if yes to all of this, is Lean Six Sigma the best way to approach the problem? Does it naturally fit into one of the four categories described in Chapter One? Is the business objective to improve quality, reduce risk, reduce cycle time, and/or improve capacity? Is the solution to the problem really unknown? Answering those questions should help you, the coach, to test whether the problem is big and interesting enough to provide a satisfying return on investment to the business sponsor and to the Belt-to-be.

But on the other hand, you should also test whether the scope is small enough to be manageable within a short and impactful Lean Six Sigma initiative. Is defining, understanding, and resolving the problem manageable in a six- to eight-month timeframe? Is it too complex to be managed by someone who is learning along the way? Are you confident the journey will eventually provide a positive experience of Lean Six Sigma to the Green or Black Belt as well as to the business's stakeholders?

In brief, you, the coach, are responsible for ensuring that the initiative and the people committed to it gather to bring the Lean Six Sigma initiative to a happy end. It can be summarized by truly, honestly, and constructively answering one single question: *would you, yourself, lead or sponsor this Lean Six Sigma initiative with these people as your project resources if you were the project manager?*

And if your own personal answer is "No," do not let a Lean Six Sigma project start! Lean Six Sigma is not the only way to approach problems and projects. Think again and choose an adapted method, even if the right method is not the one that was first considered. I bet you would not start climbing the 8091-meter-high Annapurna without a minimum of physical preparation, a good sleeping bag to keep you warm at night in a tent laid on ice, and a trustworthy mountain guide, so why would you start a Lean Six Sigma journey if you are less than 95 percent confident it is going to be successful, leaving a positive impression for the people who lived it with you? It would be unfair to expect the Belts-to-be, who are supposed to learn the methodology from you, to untie some knots that you would not untie yourself, pretending they will be able to do it as they know the business environment better. Though the Belts-to-be are responsible for delivering on the Lean Six Sigma initiative, you, the coach, are accountable for checking beforehand that the quality of the ground will accommodate a successful journey. As Abraham Lincoln said, "*You cannot escape the responsibility of tomorrow by evading it today.*"

The second aspect of the preparation phase is the theoretical training. A Lean Six Sigma journey is made of theoretical training and practice. I believe Green or Black Belts-to-be are well armed to practically begin the Lean Six Sigma initiative only after acquiring the end-to-end vision of what to expect from Define to Control.

Have you ever noticed that a track looks shorter and easier when you know how long it is and where and when to turn? Do you feel more comfortable driving when you have a map and envision the route from the start, or when you are told to take a left turn one hundred meters before the crossing?

All recognized Black and Master Black Belts have had to manage impatient stakeholders who want to jump to the endgame from the start. Belts-to-be cannot be asked to manage such stakeholders if they do not have the visibility from the beginning that the Engineer / Improve phase, during which the improvements are actually delivered, comes toward the end, for example. Providing the end-to-end vision from the start helps learners understand which path they are walking, taking the steps one after the other and managing stakeholders' expectations. And that is why the training should come first. It will tremendously help the learner to manage the pace of the journey, be patient when needed, and be filled with more Positive Energy to overcome challenges when they come by knowing the reward is just behind the corner. This does not mean that successful journeys are impossible when begun before the theoretical training, but I believe an end-to-end vision from the start helps to soothe the difficulty of the track.

Good Lean Six Sigma training should provide a few landmarks: a deep and interiorized understanding of the three pillars of a Lean Six Sigma initiative (Define, Understand, Resolve); the sequence and articulations of the five phases, including when and how to move from one phase to another; and the key tools to be used in each phase that I call hotspots. In the Define phase, the hotspots consist of project charter, SIPOC (Suppliers, Inputs, Process, Outputs, Customers) and Voice Of Customer (VOC) to Critical-To-Quality (CTQ). In the Measure phase, they are process mapping, Value Stream Analysis, Failure Modes Effects Analysis (FMEA), Cost Of Poor Quality (COPQ), and process capability. In the Analyze phase, the inevitable Five Why's. In the Engineer / Improve phase:

Brainstorming and solution selection matrix. And finally in the Control phase, the documentation, training and Control Plan. We will further explore all these tools and the mind-sets behind them in the rest of this chapter, but my point here is to emphasize that if Belts-to-be come out of a week of training with the interiorized vision of the roadmap and a good understanding of these hotspots, I bet they will be armed with the good toolbox necessary for a successful journey, even if Lean Six Sigma offers more that will be learned further along the road. Having interiorized this end-to-end vision is also a great motivation factor, giving a meaning to the life to be lived.

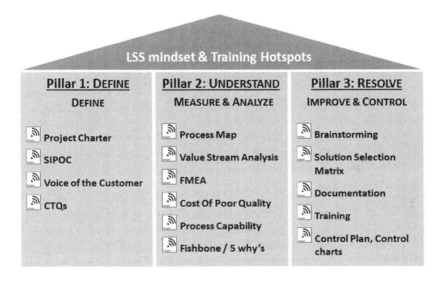

Once you, the coach, are confident the ground is ready—that you have a good "case" where a Lean Six Sigma initiative is likely to provide value to the business, that the business stakeholders and Belt-to-be are enthusiastic and eager to take on the challenge, and that the Belt-to-be is trained and equipped with a well-balanced suitcase—only then are you ready to begin the Lean Six Sigma initiative.

As a guide to help you identify potentially successful opportunities for Lean Six Sigma development journeys, some illustrative examples follow: one example of each type of objective (case studies 1 through 4) and one example combining several typical objectives (case study 5).

CASE STUDY #1
Company XYZ: Quality Improvement

Background information:
Company XYZ is a well-placed financial institution on the market with a record number of stock transactions traded daily. It is present in three financial hubs: Tokyo, London, and New York. High transaction volumes are initiated in Tokyo and New York, yet their headquarters are located in London, where the profit and loss is aggregated: To be accounted in the daily profit at its value as traded on the market, a trade must be transferred to a London accounting book within the same day (in London hours). Such a transfer is technically represented in Company XYZ's systems via an "internal transaction" between the location where the trade is initiated and London. If the transfer to London is inaccurate, the daily profit is wrong in the system; if it is late, the profit is computed by the system with the following day's market rates and is hence inaccurate in the accounting books compared to the profit actually made on the market. Thus, the timeliness and accuracy of the inputs in the systems of the internal transactions between Tokyo or New York and London are critical to the accuracy of the company's daily profit monitoring.

Most of these internal transactions are automatically created in the London system at the input of the Tokyo and New York transactions. Yet some transactions remain in the system queue at the end of London's day, pending a manual validation; some are inaccurately created in London system, and the inaccuracies are only identified a few days later. All of this results in a gap between the profit displayed in the systems and the actual profit realized by the company; the team in London also spends a huge amount of time identifying and correcting the inaccuracies.

Coaching discussion:
As the main symptom of the "pain" in the process is likely to be felt as the time spent by the London teams identifying and correcting the inaccuracies in the internal transaction inputs, the problem is likely to be presented from there. Let's imagine the process owner in charge

of the London reconciliation team complains about this non-value-added workload and approaches you, as the Lean Six Sigma expert, seeking help and advice.

Process Owner (PO): "My team is spending two hours daily correcting system errors. I need this process to be automated."

LSS Coach (LSSC): "You have people in your team, and their responsibility is to reconcile those transactions. Why is it a problem for your team to spend two hours daily doing this? Your people are supposed to work around eight hours every day, right? Why would you need this to be automated, considering automation has a cost as well?"

PO: "The reconciliation is always performed late in the day, as New York trades are inputted late in London's time zone, and the people are working overtime."

LSSC: "Are you saying the problem is the amount of time spent in correcting system errors or the fact that the team works late?"

PO: "Both! If the transactions were booked correctly, the team would finish their work on time."

LSSC: "So if I hear you correctly, are you now saying that the problem comes from the errors in the trade inputs?"

PO: "Yes!"

LSSC: "So, am I right to say that such errors are a problem because they make your team spend time correcting system errors and working late?"

PO: "Yes!"

LSSC: "Is overtime the only reason why these errors are a real problem for your team?"

PO: "No. For Tokyo transactions, because of the time difference, we even have to wait until the next day to investigate and resolve the errors with the local team. But my team objective is to clear all errors at the end of London's day, so it looks really bad for us to have some errors left unexplained at the end of the system day."

Lessons learned:

The process owner complains about the *symptoms* of the problem and approaches the problem thinking about what seems an obvious solution to him: automation.

His concerns are focused on *time spent* correcting defects and *overtime* in the teams.

Yet the essence of the problem lies in the number of defects (late or inaccurate inputs) rather than overtime and lack of automation: the objective should be to reduce the number of defects (i.e., internal transactions not inputted correctly and timely in the London system). Reducing overtime and corrections will be one of the benefits coming as a consequence of reducing the errors.

Whether automation is the best solution is a question to be kept for the Improve phase and is hence challenged by the coach up front and left aside for the rest of the discussion.

The coach drives the discussion toward the core of the *problem* rather than the way to resolve it.

The self-reflective questions help the process owner to answer himself the critical questions, allowing for the identification of good opportunities: What is the problem? *Errors in the trade inputs.* Why is it a problem? *Time spent in investigations and corrections and failure in meeting performance objective.* How do I know it really is a problem? *Overtime and bad performance indicators.* The fact that the process owner jumps to automation as a way to resolve the problem (the greatest temptation for most process owners) shows he does not have a robust process solution in mind, most likely because he has not really identified the root causes of the problem.

As the problem is linked to a high number of defects and is really a problem that must be resolved yet is without a known method for simply and realistically resolving it, the process owner has naturally spotted a good opportunity for a quality improvement Lean Six Sigma project. The improvement goal should be to reduce the number of trade input errors; the watchdog goal should be to avoid increasing the team size and workload.

CASE STUDY #2
Company ABC: Risk Reduction

Background information:
Company ABC is growing rapidly, expanding its business in a few emerging countries in parallel while keeping its production well grounded into its headquarter country. Company ABC mainly sells physical goods in the local currency of each country yet bills most of its expenses in its headquarters' currency: HQD (Headquarter Dollar).

In order to protect itself against the fluctuations of the HQD, Company ABC buys the local currency via forex transactions in the different countries when the production of the physical goods starts, transactions highly scrutinized by each local regulator keen on avoiding large corporations to speculate in their markets.

A failure in sending timely and accurate information to each regulator would result in the loss of the license for selling goods in the country.

So, in order to provide timely and accurate information to the regulators, the person in charge of sending it (the process owner) asks two persons to produce the same information and to ensure they come up with the same numbers. If not, the two persons check with each other and consolidate the final information to be sent together. When such verifications have to be made, the two people struggle to prepare the information on time.

Coaching discussion:
It is a typical scenario where the process owner compensates his fear of not meeting regulatory requirements by duplicating the work. Here again, the obvious symptom seen by the process owner is the high workload on the team. Furthermore, even though the information has always been sent on time, with no regulatory sanction for being inaccurate, the process owner never feels truly confident the information is going to be out timely and accurately. So he approaches you as the Lean Six Sigma expert to seek help and advice.

Process Owner (PO): "I have had enough of these two people spending their time consolidating all this information for the regulators. There are so many other things to do; it is a pure waste of time! But I have no choice, or our business will close."

Lean Six Sigma Coach (LSSC): "Why are you asking two of them to do the same tasks and control one another? Are they too junior to be trusted for consolidating the information correctly?"

PO: "No, they are very senior resources. But I need to ensure the information is correct!"

LSSC: "Why duplicate the work?"

PO: "Because it is a very manual process. If they come up with the same results, I am pretty sure it is correct. And if not, they can find out together which one is right. Two levels of checking are always safer."

LSSC: "Do you really need to duplicate the entire process? Is it really 'two levels' or twice the same level? Are there any critical tasks in which you have seen most errors arising?"

PO: "Frankly, I have never looked at the actual errors made during the process. I trust them to give me the accurate information to be sent in the end, once they come up with a data set both of them agree with."

LSSC: "Do you know how often they come up with the same results the first time?"

PO: "Looking at the amount of discussions they hold together, I bet it is not very often."

LSSC: "So are you saying the information has to be almost systematically analyzed before being trusted, yet you have never really seen any situation when the final report is late or inaccurate?"

PO: "Yes. We cannot afford the information to be late or inaccurate, but it takes us a lot of effort to make it right. And I am always afraid there is a chance it could be wrong: The only way is for me to trust them for their expertise and teamwork and to double the checks."

Lessons learned:

Here again, the process owner complains about the *symptoms* of the problem: duplication of tasks, waste of time and resources.

Yet the essence of the problem lies in the fact that the process is not robust enough; it has a lot of variations not understood by the process owner.

The process owner compensates his fear of inaccuracy by over-processing, with the intention of increasing the level of control. He is confident over-processing helps to increase control, as he has never received any complaint that the report is inaccurate: no defect, but the constant fear of seeing some. It is surely a way to increase control, but does it truly reduce the process risk?

It is a typical example where defects cannot be measured, yet the risk inherent to the current process should be analyzed so that the controls can be focused on where processing errors are more likely to happen. Once the process is strengthened where needed (only), duplication of work can be stopped while increasing the confidence in the accuracy of the information, eventually reducing the risk of delay due to required investigations. All in all, it means effectively reducing the process risk while eliminating the wastes in the current process.

The coach, here also, orients the discussion toward the core of the problem. The self-reflective questions guide the process owner to himself define the problem (*always a chance the information could be wrong*), to explain why it is a problem for him (*risk of sending wrong or late information compelling the stop of the business, waste of time and resources*), and to express how he knows it truly is a problem (*Looking at the amount of discussions they hold together…; I have no choice, as we cannot afford the information to be wrong or late*). The fact that he lets the process run this way, while consciously aware of the "pain," shows that he does not know how to resolve the problem—here again, most likely because he does not transparently capture the root causes, the process owner remains a victim of the symptoms of the problem.

With a problem related to risk that the process may fail even though it has not yet failed, and considering that the process owner cannot afford to let the process fail but does not know how to mitigate the risks without over-processing, a Lean Six Sigma project aimed at reducing critical process risks comes naturally into shape. The project should result in making the process safe and stable.

CASE STUDY #3
Company TUV: Cycle Time Reduction

Background information:
Company TUV is running a global business with clients all around the world and call centers and client support operations located in Manila (Philippines), Wroclaw (Poland), and Raleigh (USA). The management takes great pride in being able to provide an answer to any client request in less than twelve hours, thanks to their worldwide coverage. If the client's requests are not answered within twelve hours or not resolved within forty-eight hours, the company commits to sending vouchers to their unsatisfied clients, eventually resulting in effective dollar loss for the company.

Several clients have complained in the past weeks for not seeing their requests answered in a timely manner, and Company TUV's profit has been highly affected. The management has asked the process owner to eradicate any client complaint, as well as to provide special support to the clients who have complained.

Coaching discussion:
The process owner feels a high pressure from his management to meet client expectations. He wants to understand why some clients' requests have been answered late while avoiding pressure on the teams who need to keep their client focus. He approaches you, as the Lean Six Sigma expert, seeking help and advice.

Process Owner (PO): "I really do not know what happened with these few clients. Nothing has changed recently in the process, and several clients have not been satisfied in a short period of time. What should I do?"

Lean Six Sigma Coach (LSSC): "Why did the clients raise complaints?"

PO: "I am not sure yet. The complaints come from North American clients. It is difficult for me to monitor the operations, as I sit in Europe's time zone, many kilometers away from them."

LSSC: "What is the biggest problem you are facing now: unhappy clients or lack of understanding as to why clients are unsatisfied?"

PO: "Both. I need to find out the latter to understand the former."

LSSC: "What can make clients unsatisfied?"

PO: "Our company commitment is to provide answers within twelve hours and resolve the queries within forty-eight hours; the clients' dissatisfaction is likely to come from one or the other."

LSSC: "So, are you saying that the problem comes from the delay in either answering or resolving the clients' queries and that you have been made aware of it by the clients' complaints themselves?"

PO: "Yes."

LSSC: "How far behind the deadline have the clients been attended?"

PO: "I do not know. I think I need to find this out first indeed, and then gain a better understanding of the current process timelines. From there, I should be able to see where the problem comes from."

Lessons learned:

Starting again from the symptom of the problem felt by the process owner (clients are complaining), the self-reflective questions guide him to understand why such symptoms are apparent.

The problem in this scenario revolves around timeliness: committed timelines are not met, making the problem naturally oriented toward the lack of timeliness.

The process owner realizes he needs to understand the nature and size of the gap before being able to resolve the symptoms, starting with a timeliness problem as opposed to a solution: typical opportunity for a Lean Six Sigma initiative aiming at reducing cycle time.

From the process owner's point of view, the concerns stem from the symptoms (complaints and pressure from the management); yet the questions help him to refocus on the three fundamental questions: What is the problem? *Delay in answering or resolving clients' queries.* Why is it a problem? *The company is committed to answering within twelve hours and to resolving within forty-eight hours.* How does he know it really is a problem? *Client complaints and pressure from management.* However, he seems to have no clue how to reduce the cycle time.

A business problem related to too long a cycle time, a true problem that must be resolved, without a known solution: the natural option is to run a Lean Six Sigma project aiming at reducing the cycle time.

CASE STUDY #4
Company DEF: Capacity Increase

Background information:
Company DEF is a financial institution managing large clients' portfolios. Most clients are very active on the market, having several hundreds of transactions executed every month. In order to follow their assets and liabilities accurately, the clients rely on the company to send account statements within the first three days of each month.

With a highly volatile and growing market, the number of transactions is increasing month after month, and company DEF teams are struggling to cope with transaction volume growth: Some important clients have complained about receiving late and inaccurate statements.

Coaching discussion for the Preparation phase:
The process owner has received some clients' complaints directly. On top of not meeting his performance objectives, he is afraid some key clients might escalate to management. He approaches you, as the Lean Six Sigma expert, seeking help and advice.

Process Owner (PO): "I have received some warnings from some of our clients, who've complained about our support. It is true: We have not sent the statements on time, but we have had record transactions volumes this month. My team is just overwhelmed, but I have no budget at all to hire anyone this year. And, of course, the clients will not accept being served after some other clients we judge to be more critical."

Lean Six Sigma Coach (LSSC): "What did the clients complain about?"

PO: "Some complained about late statements; others complained about errors in the statements."

LSSC: "Why are the statements sent with errors or late?"

PO: "The teams are stretched, so they make mistakes…and, of course, what cannot be sent on time is sent after the deadline."

LSSC: "So are you saying that the problem is about the amount of statements the team has to manage, and the delay and errors are the consequence of the team being overloaded?"

PO: "Yes!"

LSSC: "How do you know the overload is the problem?"

PO: "Everyone is very dedicated to doing a good job, and the job is well done in lower-volume months. It is a fact: When the teams have time, they work well."

LSSC: "If the clients are usually satisfied when volumes allow the team to do the job properly, would the clients accept receiving the statements within four or five days instead of three then?"

PO: "I do not think so. It is a market practice to send them within three days. We would risk losing clients if we did so."

Lessons learned:

The process owner starts with the symptoms of the problem: here again, client complaints.

Even though the clients complain about timeliness and accuracy of the account statements, the process owner seems confident that the true problem is about volumes and process capacity.

The self-reflective questions help the process owner express what the problem is (*overload due to volume growth*) in spite of its visible symptoms (*lack of timeliness and accuracy*), why it is a problem (*market practice not met, hence risk of losing business*), and how he knows it really is a problem (*deadlines not met, statements sent with errors, client complaints*).

With relevant answers to these three questions, and considering that the process owner does not seem to know how to simply and realistically resolve the problem, he has naturally identified himself the opportunity of a Lean Six Sigma project aimed at improving process capacity in order to absorb business growth with the same resources.

CASE STUDY #5
Company H: Hybrid

Background information:
Company H is a highly profitable business very close to its clients that takes a lot of pride in the closeness of its client relationships. The management continuously self-evaluates its image by participating in external surveys. Though Company H has always been ranked in the top three within the most popular surveys, it has recently lost its position, being ranked #7 in the latest survey.

Management sets coming back in the top three within the year as a global company objective. The client relationship manager (CRM, process owner in charge of direct client interactions) is asked to define the key actions to be implemented for the company to meet its target.

Businesswise, Company H is in charge of running short- to medium-term missions for their clients in a wide range of areas requiring different skill sets. When a client approaches Company H, the CRM confers with the client, decides whether the mission is worth the cost and effort for Company H, finds out whether people with the skills required to run the mission are available, and if not, on-boards the relevant people. If Company H agrees to run the mission, the CRM then provides quotes and timelines to the clients. The immediate availability of people to run the mission has a direct impact on the timeline and the ability of Company H to start the mission for the client. The clients usually expect an answer within two to three days (standard market practice) or they will turn to a competitor to run the mission. Furthermore, on-boarding resources has a cost for Company H, eventually making a mission costly to the company, yet this additional cost is not charged to the clients as Company H wants to remain competitive compared to other companies with broader skill sets.

In the past couple of months, in order to avoid losing business opportunities when overwhelmed by increasing client demands, a few missions have been accepted for some clients before a comprehensive review of the skill sets to be sourced. This has resulted in some missions running beyond time and budget, as Company H has not been able to provide the adequate resources and/or deliver the missions within the initially agreed upon timeline.

Coaching discussion:
The process owner is worried about being assigned a global objective in which the involvement of all teams is likely to be needed, whereas he is only in charge of the clients relationships. He approaches you, as the Lean Six Sigma expert, seeking help and advice.

Process Owner (PO): "I am asked to drive the company to meet a global target, but I am not a decision maker in all areas. Even though my team is facing the clients, it is not my responsibility if the upstream operations are not meeting client expectations."

Lean Six Sigma Coach (LSSC): "Why do you think management has asked you and not someone else?"

PO: "I guess it is because my team is interacting with the clients, and they see me responsible for their satisfaction."

LSSC: "Does *'responsible for the clients' satisfaction'* mean that you have to be responsible for all the processes in the company?"

PO: "Of course not, but at least the processes directly impacting the clients."

LSSC: "Who is the best person to understand what clients expect from the company?"

PO: "I guess it is me, as I am in charge of the team interacting with clients."

LSSC: "So could we imagine that you define the criteria critical to satisfying the customers and let each team decide how to make it relevant in their own area?"

PO: "Yes, that would be a good start."

LSSC: "Great. Remember to on-board all the key stakeholders early though, or you would very quickly be left alone in a dead end.

In the meantime, do you have an idea why client satisfaction has dropped, based on the results of the surveys?"

PO: "I have a few things in mind. Some clients are not satisfied because we are not meeting the deadlines we signed up for; they are right, but I do not have the resources! I can't do anything, even though I take the blame!"

LSSC: "Why do you think the deadlines are not being met, even though the company has committed to them at the start of the mission?"

PO: "We are short on resources to both scope and execute missions. Regarding scoping, I cannot secure all resources in less than three days before accepting missions, and I cannot afford to decline or lose some missions promising a good payoff. Regarding execution, the resources I initially relied on have been assigned to other missions the company could not afford to reject or fail."

LSSC: "Why did not you on-board more resources instead of simply reassigning them? Isn't it better to bear a small extra cost at the end of your mission, rather than having an entire mission seen as a failure in the client's eyes?"

PO: "Agreed! But the resources have been taken from me without notice, Time to anticipate and on-board new people, we are beyond committed timelines."

LSSC: "Were not you aware of this new critical mission starting in parallel?"

PO: "I did. But I had no way to figure out early enough which resources would have to be re-assigned."

LSSC: "So, are you saying the problem is actually the lack of transparency and communication on committing the resources, rather than lack of time and resources?"

PO: "Yes, somehow it can be said so."

LSSC: "Alright, so, in brief, it seems you pretty much know what the problems are: inability to provide timely and accurate answer to clients when scoping missions, and delays in executing missions committed to clients."

Lessons learned:

The problem starts with a business challenge: a bad rank in a survey as the result of many teams working in parallel without proper communication and connections enabling the articulation of a streamlined front-to-back process.

Once again, the process owner feels the symptoms of the problems: Management makes him painfully aware of the importance of the problem.

The self-reflective questions guide him to break down the business challenge (*bad rank in the survey*) into more tangible and concrete symptoms (*lack of transparency on resources immediately available to source the mission, delay in client deliveries*), which represent the essence of the problem and force him to explain why it really is a problem to him (*My clients are not satisfied because we are not meeting their deadlines*).

As the CRM does not know how to straightforwardly resolve the problem, he naturally comes to the need of a Lean Six Sigma project aimed at improving quality (reducing defects: missions not executed as committed to clients), reducing process risk (risk for not delivering missions as committed to clients), and reducing the cycle time for scoping missions (cycle time from reception of clients' requests to answering back with a "yes" or "no").

> Typical first-level self-reflective questions:
> - What is the problem?
> - Why is it a problem that needs to be fixed?
> - How do you know it truly is a problem?
> - Do you have an idea of how the problem could be resolved?

The rest of this chapter focuses on how to practically walk along the road, week after week (remember, we agreed to guide Belts-to-be on a weekly basis), ensuring an almost systematically successful journey.

As some coaching discussions are likely to follow a very similar format from one project to another, a detailed discussion is given as an illustrative example of how to drive questions and answer them and of which outcomes to expect, topic by topic. We will use Case Study #5 as the underlying background. The illustrative discussion, referred to as the *"framed discussion,"* is represented in a frame, isolated from the rest of the journey to help the reader separate the typical flow and guidelines from the illustration. This *framed discussion* is to be taken as an easily reproducible illustration. However, as some sessions are too highly dependent on the contents of the project rather than its framework, the *framed discussion* is sometimes omitted: it is only proposed when relevant and straightforwardly replicable in another context.

Define

A problem well stated is a problem half solved.

The Define mind-set

As obvious as it might be, the essence of the Define phase is to properly define the problem, which brings Belts-to-be half-way through its resolution. A process improvement project starts with a *problem* (in opposition to a *solution*) often only vaguely expressed at the start. The Define phase ends once the business problem has been translated into a list of specific and measurable key success factors driven by customers' expectations, and validated by the sponsor. Defining a clear and transparent end state sets the contract between Belt-to-be and sponsor.

As the coach, this summary of the Define phase is what you must inject into the brain of Belts-to-be all along the Define phase to help them grasp Pillar One of the Lean Six Sigma mind-set. They must keep in mind this objective of defining CTQs (Critical-To-Quality) to be signed off by the sponsor in the Define tollgate.

Template: the conclusions of the Define phase
Completing the Define phase should lead to filling in the following template where the text in *italic* is given as an illustration:

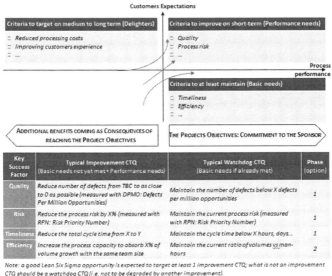

Customers Expectations

Criteria to target on medium to long term (Delighters)	Criteria to improve on short-term (Performance needs)
☐ Reduced processing costs ☐ Improving customers experience ☐ ...	☐ Quality ☐ Process risk ☐ ...

Process performance

Criteria to at least maintain (Basic needs)

☐ Timeliness
☐ Efficiency
☐ ...

| ADDITIONAL BENEFITS COMING AS CONSEQUENCES OF REACHING THE PROJECT OBJECTIVES | THE PROJECTS OBJECTIVES: COMMITMENT TO THE SPONSOR |

Key Success Factor	Typical Improvement CTQ (Basic needs not yet met + Performance needs)	Typical Watchdog CTQ (Basic needs if already met)	Phase (option)
Quality	Reduce number of defects from TBC to as close to 0 as possible (measured with DPMO: Defects Per Million Opportunities)	Maintain the number of defects below X defects per million opportunities	1
Risk	Reduce the process risk by X% (measured with RPN: Risk Priority Number)	Maintain the current process risk (measured with RPN: Risk Priority Number)	1
Timeliness	Reduce the total cycle time from X to Y	Maintain the cycle time below X hours, days...	1
Efficiency	Increase the process capacity to absorb X% of volume growth with the same team size	Maintain the current ratio of volumes vs man-hours	2

Note: a good Lean Six Sigma opportunity is expected to target at least 1 improvement CTQ; what is not an improvement CTQ should be a watchdog CTQ (i.e. not to be degraded by another improvement).

Week 1: Project charter and SIPOC

Expect Belts-to-be to come to the session with a draft of a project charter, having committed to paper some ideas for an opportunity statement, goal statement, business case, project scope, project team, and project plan. Also ask them to prepare a draft SIPOC before the session, highlighting the boundaries of the scope of the process.

Work with them on improving the contents of the charter and SIPOC if need be, especially opportunity and goal statements, critical components to lay the foundations of a safe start.

Then, move on to the next steps and analyze the challenges to expect. From the SIPOC, question Belts-to-be on the customers: Who are they? How difficult is it to reach out to them and to collect their voice? Which method (among Learn, Ask, Watch, Do) will be best adapted to collecting it? Many Belts-to-be tend to orientate the VOC collection around what is expected from the *project* rather than from the *process:* warn them of this common pitfall; ensure they capture the sponsor's expectations (project point of view) independently from customers' expectations (process point of view), not solely concentrating on what could be improved (setting the improvement goals), but also on what works well that must not be degraded at the expense of any other improvement (setting the "watchdog" goals). Agree with Belts-to-be on a timeline to complete the collection of the VOC: it should be completed within a week, two at most, prior to the next coaching session.

In this first session, also introduce the need to outline the main milestones of the project plan, not as a constraint but as a tool to self-evaluate and transparently challenge the progress of the project. Discuss with Belts-to-be the method they will adopt to structure regular communication with key stakeholders on progress and risks identified along the project: weekly/biweekly updates, short updates in a pre-existing governance—it depends on the stakeholders. Belts must choose which method will be most easily adapted to the context and people, but they must be convinced that consistent communication by regularly informing stakeholders of progress made is key in maintaining their interest. Project risk management also benefits when Belts anticipate potential project roadblocks as early as possible and keep stakeholders aware of them, preparing them to be involved in the event that a decision or arbitration is required.

At the end of this session, Belts-to-be must have learned some key Lean Six Sigma hardware (tools): project charter, SIPOC, and VOC collection. Most of this should have been captured during the training, and the role of the coach is to fill in the remaining gaps, if any, and to outline the objectives and outcomes of such tools.

Belts must have learned basic project management aspects as well, such as drafting a basic project plan articulated around DMAEC / DMAIC, identifying and on-boarding stakeholders, and communicating on risks identified in the project.

In terms of software (Lean Six Sigma mind-set), Belts-to-be must grasp the importance of defining scope and objectives up front, in line with both sponsor and customers expectations.

Send the EN-E-RG-IZ-E summary before the end of the day, encouraging on what has been accomplished and recapitulating the next steps with positive actions: refine the charter and SIPOC if needed, collect the VOC, and communicate with the stakeholders.

Typical first-level self-reflective questions to be asked by the coach and meaningfully answered by the Belt-to-be (in the language of the business):

- What is the problem?
- Why is it a problem, making you confident you have a case?
- Who is impacted by the problem?
- When and where is the problem happening?
- How big is the problem?
- Would you be able to provide a few numbers demonstrating how severe the problem is?
- How do you know there is a problem worth fixing?
- Are the objectives SMART?
- How do you measure risk?
- How do you measure quality (or accuracy)?
- At what point do you consider the objectives met and the project a success?
- How are you going to convince the sponsor the project is worth the effort?
- To what extent is the problem a roadblock to meeting the strategic objectives of the company?
- How big are the financial and nonfinancial benefits to expect?
- What is the scope of the project?
- What is out of scope?
- Are all potentially impacted parties represented in the project team?
- Is everyone aware of what is expected from them? Is everyone committed to the goal?
- Who is enthusiastic?
- Who is likely to resist? Why?
- Who could influence opponents if need be?
- Are there external factors already known to pose a risk to the project deliverables and timeline?
- What are the boundaries of the process in scope?

- Who are the customers of the process (internal & external)?
- Are all process outputs needed by at least one customer?
- Can you identify any quick win (easy/cheap process change bringing benefits and easily reversible) from the high-level process description?

Framed Discussion

The Client Relationship Manager from Company H (process owner and Belt-to-be) is expected to come to the session with a draft project charter and SIPOC. Following the preparation discussion he had with the coach, the opportunity is likely to be around dissatisfied clients and his inability to properly and adequately source missions to deliver as committed; the objectives are likely to be around providing an answer to clients within three days (whether Company H is going to run the mission or not) and meeting client deadlines as committed; the business case is likely to be around improving client satisfaction and avoiding lost business.

LSSC: "Hi! What's up today?"

Belt (B): "Well, I have started my project charter and SIPOC. I would like to review them with you and see what the next steps will be."

LSSC: "Great start! Tell me more; explain your project charter."

B: "Starting with the opportunity, I have described the nature of the problem: clients are not satisfied by our service, as we've failed to deliver some missions as per our commitment."

LSSC: "Good start. That answers two of the fundamental questions—*what the problem is and why it is a problem*—making you confident you have a case. How about the other questions laying the opportunity statement framework: Who is impacted by the problem? When and where is the problem happening? How big is the problem? Would you be able to provide a few numbers here, demonstrating how severe the problem is?"

B: "I should be able to determine how many clients have complained and how late the missions were indeed. I will add that, as well as the answers to the other questions structuring the opportunity."

LSSC: "Good. How about the goal then?"

B: "I have set two objectives: timeliness—provide an answer whether we run the mission or not to all our clients requests in less than three days, and quality—complete all missions as committed to the clients."

LSSC: "Good start! Do you remember the characteristics of 'good' objectives?"

B: "SMART?"

LSSC: "Yes. Are your objectives SMART?"

B: "Specific and Measurable: yes. Achievable and Realistic: I think so. Time-bounded: fair enough; let me add the timeline."

LSSC: "*Achievable and Realistic...you think so.* How could you be convinced? Will you still consider it a success if one mission out of one hundred is completed behind deadline, or if one answer to one client is given in four days?"

B: "Can I decide that later?"

LSSC: "Yes and no. Yes, as the charter is a living document that you can keep updating if you think the environment requires it. That will require the sponsor to agree though. But no, as, at some point, you must decide what success means. How could you capture this buffer zone between commitment and uncertainty?"

B: "Maybe by wording the objectives in a less determined way? Something like 'answers provided beyond three days to be as close to zero as possible,' and measuring the performance with the DPMO (Defects Per Million of Opportunities) of answers not provided within three days."

LSSC: "Indeed, that would give you some buffer zone. But then, what does 'as possible' mean in specific and measurable terms?"

B: "I do not get you. How can the goals be specific and measurable and at the same time allow a buffer zone?"

LSSC: "What if the 'buffer' was translated into a risk-reduction objective?"

B: "Ah, OK. So you are saying I should define the objective with a buffer zone and at the same time set an objective of reducing the risk of not meeting the deadlines?"

LSSC: "Why not?"

B: "So, the timeliness and quality objectives become nuanced by 'as close to zero as possible' ('close' measured with DPMO), and I add one objective to reduce the process risk."

LSSC: "Very good! How are you going to measure the risk and define the goal in specific and measurable terms then?"

B: "Good question. Recollecting the learning from the training, I could measure the current risk with an FMEA (Failure Modes Effects Analysis), using the RPN (Risk Priority Number) as the metric and target to reduce the RPN to as close to zero as possible."

LSSC: "It sounds great! What would the business case look like then?"

B: "The benefits will be about improving client satisfaction and better managing our business requests."

LSSC: "Would you be able to measure financial benefits from there? Either additional costs avoided by not on-boarding additional resources or additional profit from new business?"

B: "It seems challenging, as it means forecasting the volume of client requests we will be receiving."

LSSC: "What if the sponsor does not give you the resources to run this initiative? How can you convince him there is a real benefit?"

B: "Well, seen under this angle, I guess I can try to make some estimates based on how many requests we currently have and extrapolate from there."

LSSC: "Yes, that is important. Giving some figures in the business case (and not in the goal statement) does not commit you directly but helps you convince yourself as well as the other stakeholders of the importance of running the project. And we never know, you might find the project is not worth it if the "pain" is not worth fixing. On top of the financial benefits, you are right: list the expected benefits for the clients and for the company as a whole in managing the requests more efficiently and accurately."

B: "Great. So, we now have opportunity, goal, and business case. Moving on to the scope of the project, I need to look at all clients within my perimeter; I have excluded clients managed by other managers."

LSSC: "Good. That makes sense. Your proposal can be replicated later on if successful, but indeed, let's limit this specific project to where you can make direct decisions. How about the perimeter of the process?"

B: "I need to include the entire process."

LSSC: "What does 'entire' mean? Are you also going to look at how client payments are recorded by the accounting department, for example?"

B: "No, I mean the entire process from my end. OK, I get it. I have to specify the first and last steps of the process I intend to improve."

LSSC: "Which tool have you learned for representing the boundaries of the process?"

B: "SIPOC. OK, let's look at what I have started to prepare then. I have listed the suppliers and inputs, macro process steps, outputs, and customers."

LSSC: "It looks good. Are you able to link all outputs to at least one customer from the list?"

B: "It seems one of the outputs of the process is a client statement that nobody is using anymore, since we have put in place a new team sending bills to clients."

LSSC: "Oh. Why are we still preparing these statements then?"

B: "I guess there is no point."

LSSC: "It seems you have a quick win then! Let's stop producing such statements. What else did you learn from the SIPOC?"

B: "It helps me to understand where the process I am in charge of starts and ends, as well as to list the dependencies from suppliers and inputs, and to list my customers. I figured out that the external clients are not the only customers of the process."

LSSC: "Excellent! So, back to your charter, you now have the project and process scope. How about the project team?"

B: "The sponsor is going to be my manager concerned about client complaints. I am the process owner as well as the project manager."

LSSC: "Is there anybody else you need to involve who could potentially be impacted by the project?"

B: "Yes, you're right. I should also on-board the teams sourcing my missions. I will add one representative of each skill set team I usually work with. "

LSSC: "Good. And finally, the project plan?"

B: "I have set the timeline with about one month per phase."

LSSC: "Good. Are you anticipating any specific event that might put this project work on hold for any specific reason?"

B: "No, it is my priority to get this done. I will make it come first."

LSSC: "Good. Now that you have charter and SIPOC, what's next?"

B: "Recollecting again from the training, I now need to collect the voice of the customers?"

LSSC: "Indeed. Who are your customers?"

B: "My clients."

LSSC: "Only your clients?"

B: "Ah, OK. The list is in the SIPOC."

LSSC: "Indeed. Which difficulties do you expect in collecting their voices? Are they all easily reachable? Do you already know part of their voice?"

B: "Well, I can look again at the complaints the clients have raised. And I will ask the other customers open-ended questions."

LSSC: "Excellent. That is indeed what you need to do next. When can it be done?"

B: "I guess I can speak to them within two or three weeks."

LSSC: "Will it be soon enough for you to complete the Define phase as scheduled in your project plan?"

B: "Oh…indeed, I intend to complete the Define phase within the next two to three weeks."

LSSC: "Can you collect the voices of your customers within a week, and we can work together next week to move on to the next step according to what your customers tell you."

B: "OK."

LSSC: "Good. So, in brief, within a week, try to review the charter and SIPOC as we discussed and collect the voices of all your customers regarding their expectations from the process. It is really critical that you get the customer voices before we can move forward."

Week 2: Voice of customers and CTQs

Expect Belts-to-be to come to the session with customer voices. Work with them on what they've learned from the VOC: Have the customers highlighted some process wastes or suggested some improvements that could be quick wins? What are the key concepts highlighted? All will most likely revolve around timeliness, quality, accuracy, risk, and workload. Using self-reflective questions, guide Belts-to-be to identify these categories critical to the customer, and from there, question them on how to define CTQs

(Critical-To-Quality): specific indicators allowing for measurement of customer satisfaction criteria, with a starting measurement point and a target.

Then, move to the next steps and analyze the challenges to expect. Question Belts-to-be on which CTQ is more or less important to the customer, and guide them to organize the CTQs by priority, in line with the project objectives. The Kano model is a good way to represent the VOC and CTQs in line with sponsor and customer expectations: from the basics (to be reached or maintained), to performance (improvement drivers) and delighters (what may be obtained on the longer term as a consequence of the basics and performance expectations, beyond the results solely expected from the project, and will excite the customers as they would not even have thought by themselves that such results could be delivered). Once the CTQs are defined and prioritized, Belts-to-be should start preparing the tollgate to close the Define phase.

In regard to hardware, by the end of the session, Belts-to-be must have learned how to derive CTQs from VOC and understood the Kano model.

In terms of software, they must have learned the importance of the *customer* in a Lean Six Sigma initiative as a driver for defining the end state.

Send the EN-E-RG-IZ-E summary before the end of the day, encouraging on what has been accomplished and recapitulating the next steps with positive actions: refine and finalize CTQs if needed, and prepare the Define tollgate.

Typical first-level self-reflective questions to be asked by the coach and meaningfully answered by Belts-to-be (in the language of the business):

- How did you collect the voice of the customer?
- Have you captured the voices of all the customers?
- What did your customers tell you regarding what they currently like from the process?
- What do they expect to see improved?
- What do they expect to see maintained?
- Are the customers' expectations from the *process* synergistic or antagonistic with the sponsor's expectations from the *project*?
- What is not said but intended by the customers?
- Behind each customer voice, can you identify some concepts or requirements mentioned by several customers?
- Can the different voices be grouped?
- What is critical to customer satisfaction?
- What is basic for them in the process? Are those basic expectations already met, or should they be reached as an absolute necessity?
- What would increase their satisfaction level if the process could perform better?
- What could excite or delight them on top of the basic and performance needs?
- How can we prioritize their different expectations (basic: short-term versus performance: short to medium term versus delighters: medium to long term)?
- How do we translate their voices into specific metrics? What is the current measurement level? What should be the target?

The course of this coaching discussion will highly depend on what the customers have said and what the Belt-to-be has learned from them. Therefore, the *framed discussion* is omitted here.

Week 3: Preparation of the Define tollgate

Expect Belts-to-be to come to the session with a draft of the document to be presented to the stakeholders in the tollgate.

Work with them on preparing the slides and transitions between the slides. Start with the project charter, and more specifically with catching the attention on current situation, problems, opportunities and objectives, then project scope. From the project scope, move to the SIPOC as a way to set the boundaries of the process to be improved in the project. From the customers listed in the SIPOC, move to the Kano model and the CTQs, Quick wins if any. The list of CTQs sets the end of the Define phase by defining the target end state, hence must be validated by the sponsor by the end of the tollgate. The template proposed in the section on the Define mind-set on page 53 could be the last slide, wrapping up the conclusions of the Define phase.

Most importantly, guide them on how to articulate the *story*: what is learned from which tool, what the connections are between each of them, how to transition from the outcome of one tool to the need for using the next, and how to present the progress and outcomes of the Define phase. Once the story line is clear and well articulated, Belts-to-be should schedule the Define tollgate.

Regarding hardware, Belts-to-be must have interiorized the learning and outcomes of the hotspots from the Define phase (as listed in the three-pillar diagram at the end of the training) by the end of the session.

In terms of software, they must have learned to prepare a Define tollgate meeting and understood the importance of validating the objectives and CTQs with the sponsor before moving to the Measure phase.

Send the EN-E-RG-IZ-E summary before the end of the day, encouraging on what has been accomplished and recapitulating the next steps with positive actions: refine the slides of the Define tollgate if needed, schedule the meeting, and prepare the story line.

Typical first-level self-reflective questions:

- What is the objective of the meeting?
- What is expected from the audience?
- What is the agenda?
- How does each point in the agenda convey the message and help to reach the meeting objective?
- What is the learning from each tool? Is each item worth mentioning to the stakeholders, or should the learning be considered a "working" step for the project manager only?
- What is the best way to present the charter without reading but rather highlighting what makes an impact to the audience?
- What is the link between the charter and SIPOC, and why do you present the SIPOC?
- In how much detail should the process be described (if the SIPOC is chosen to be presented)?
- Is there any interesting learning from the SIPOC to be emphasized to the stakeholders (such as quick wins)?
- What is the link between SIPOC and VOC, and why do you present the VOC?
- What is the best way to present the VOC in a concise, organized manner?
- How have the project deliverables been prioritized?
- Have you planned to ask the sponsor to approve the project and objectives as stated by the CTQs?
- Do you expect any specific questions to be raised by any of the stakeholders?

Framed Discussion

LSSC: "Hi! What's up today?"

B: "Let's prepare the Define tollgate."

LSSC: "OK. Tell me more. What have you done? What is the objective of the meeting? What do you expect from the audience? What will be the agenda?"

B: "The objective is for the sponsor to approve the project. For the agenda, I consolidated the outcomes of the Define phase: Project charter, SIPOC, Kano diagram showing the VOC and their priorities, and CTQs."

LSSC: "Good start! What is the learning from each tool? How will you articulate the message from one to the other?"

B: "I will start with the charter. Should I read everything?"

LSSC: "What do you think? What is the message you want to deliver behind the charter?"

B: "I want to explain what the problem is, how big it is, and why it is important to resolve it. I want to demonstrate to what extent the specific objectives, once achieved, will resolve the problem. I also want to highlight the broader benefits to be expected."

LSSC: "Do you think you will impact the stakeholders better by reading the charter or by preparing a short story around these few messages?"

B: "Well, I guess I should rather prepare a short, concise story to capture their attention. After that, I intend to briefly present the timeline, project team, and scope."

LSSC: "Good plan. What's next?"

B: "The SIPOC. Should I read everything to describe the process?"

LSSC: "Before moving into the contents, how do you transition to the SIPOC? In other words, what is the link between the charter and SIPOC and why do you present the SIPOC?"

B: "The SIPOC helps to define the boundaries of the process. OK, so I can transition from the scope. And provide a high-level description of the process and its boundaries."

LSSC: "Sounds good! How 'high-level' or detailed are you going to be in describing the process?"

B: "Not sure…"

LSSC: "Why do you need to provide a high-level description of the process?"

B: "So that the stakeholders visualize the extent of the project and its dependencies."

LSSC: "Indeed. How knowledgeable are the stakeholders regarding the process, and how interested are they in visualizing the process?"

B: "I think they are quite far away from the process. OK, I got it. I will stay high-level."

LSSC: "Is there any interesting learning from the SIPOC you want to emphasize to them?"

B: "It may be worth highlighting the quick win. I mean, ceasing preparation of these statements that nobody is using anymore."

LSSC: "Indeed! What's next then?"

B: "Voice of customers and Kano."

LSSC: "What is the link between SIPOC and VOC? Why do you present the VOC?"

B: "The link is with the customers. So I could read the list of customers from the SIPOC, explain how I collected their voices, and present the outcomes: basic expectations, performance needs, and delighters."

LSSC: "Good! What is the point in presenting these three categories of needs?"

B: "Explaining how to prioritize the deliverables, driven by customer expectation and satisfaction factors?"

LSSC: "Indeed! So, once the priorities are set, what's next?"

B: "CTQs. So, here, the transition is straightforward: I can explain how I translated the VOC into specific and measurable terms, critical to the success of the project."

LSSC: "Sounds good! What's next then?"

B: "The end..."

LSSC: "So how are you going to wrap up and conclude, demonstrating the meeting objective is reached and obtaining what you need from the audience?"

B: "The objective is to obtain the sponsor's sign-off, so I could first ask him if he agrees with the list of CTQs, and propose continuing with the Measure phase if he does."

LSSC: "Excellent! It sounds very good. One more thing: do you expect any specific question to be raised by any of the stakeholders?"

B: "Indeed, based on some exchanges I had with other people. Let me think about it; I will prepare the answers."

LSSC: "Good. So, in brief, before the meeting, work on articulating this story as we just did and focus on conveying the message rather than planning to show all you have done by reading the slides. It is critical that you prepare your speech to convince the audience your project is worth sponsoring."

Week 4: Debrief after the Define tollgate

Expect Belts-to-be to come to the session after sending the minutes of the Define tollgate to the stakeholders.

Debrief then on the tollgate and the Define phase as the First Pillar of the Lean Six Sigma mind-set.

Move onto the Measure phase.

Measure

A man should look for what is and not for what he thinks should be.

—Albert Einstein

The Measure mind-set

The essence of the Measure phase could be summarized in one word: baseline. Here, Belts-to-be must capture the need to understand the *process* and measure the gap with the expected end state, as defined by the CTQs from the Define tollgate. Understanding a process is not simple. "Design is not just what it looks like and feels like. Design is how it works," said Steve Jobs. Truly *understanding a process* is not just being able to draw a decision chart or a swim lane diagram or measuring an average cycle time over a significant period of time; it means truly capturing how the process *works*—how the inputs are transformed into the output. This is what Belts-to-be must understand at this stage of their development of the Lean Six Sigma mind-set.

A simple and practical way to inject this mind-set is to outline three progressive steps as outcomes of the Measure phase, starting with the visualization of the process (process mapping), continuing with the measurement of its current performance (in line with indicators set as CTQs), and ending with the measurement and illustration of the gap between the current situation and the expected end state meeting customers and sponsor expectations (process capability, or any other chart making the gap visual)

Templates: The conclusions of the Measure phase
Completing the Measure phase should lead to filling in the below templates where the text in *italic* is provided as an illustration, according to each project type:

Quality Improvement Projects:
The size of the problem: Cost Of Poor Quality

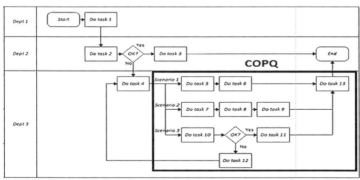

Observations (facts):
❏ *The COPQ comes from 9 tasks, triggered by defects coming out of Task 2.*
❏ *Most of the time spent in corrections is due to:*
  – *Scenario 3*
  – *Defects coming out of Task 10*
  – *Time-consuming Task 12*

Consequences:
❏ *High re-work rate: X%*
❏ *X man-hours spent in COPQ, resulting in X USD / year of unnecessary processing costs*

Risk reduction Projects:
The size of the problem: RPN from the FMEA

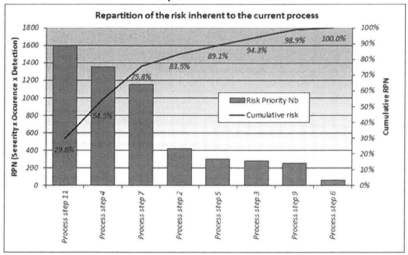

Observations (facts):

☐ *More than 75% of the risk inherent to the current process is concentrated on 3 tasks.*

☐ *Main causes for the risk inherent to the current process:*
- *Reliance on non robust tools*
- *Lack of guidelines to execute process step 4*
- *High rate of Human errors when performing process steps 4 and 7*

Consequences:

☐ *Need to duplicate 3 downstream controls*

☐ *Risk of inaccurate and late processing*

Cycle time reduction Projects:
The size of the problem:
gap between TAKT time and actual time - Value Stream Analysis

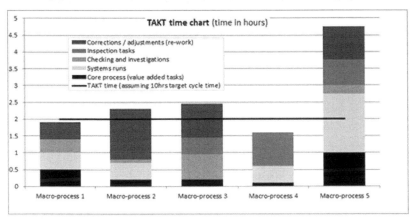

Observations (facts):
- ☐ The time spent in core processing (value-added tasks) and system runs is within the affordable time.
- ☐ 3 macros-processes are not completed within the affordable time.
- ☐ Macro-process 5 represents the greatest bottleneck.

Consequences:
- ☐ The overall cycle time is above the affordable time by X hours.
- ☐ X% of the gap is made of non-value added tasks.
- ☐ Yet the core process and system runs do not show any major constraint.

Capacity increase Projects:
The size of the problem: gap between volumes of inputs processed by 1 HC (Headcount) and expected processing volumes

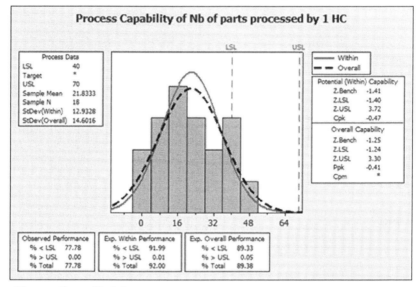

Observations (facts):
❏ *1 HC (Headcount) processes ~22 parts in average with a significant variation (~13 parts).*

Consequences:
❏ *The expected target of 40 (LSL = Lower Specification Limit) to 70 (USL = Upper Specification Limit) parts per HC is not met.*

Week 4 (cont'd): Introduction to the Measure phase, process mapping

Introduce the Measure phase and analyze the challenges to expect. Question Belts-to-be on the objectives and expected outcomes of the Measure phase in line with the specific Lean Six Sigma initiative being run. Reiterate for them the *mind-set* of the Measure phase.

Once the mind-set is understood and the path of the Measure phase visualized, Belts-to-be should walk out of this session with the mission of drafting a process map. Briefly remind them how to proceed and what makes a good process map, ensuring they will not get stuck on technical roadblocks. The typical question they will ask is how granular the map should be: remind them why a process map is needed (for analysis and not for documentation, as it is the Measure phase) and how the process map should help to visualize the CTQs, and let them start and learn on the job!

Regarding hardware, at the end of the session, Belts-to-be must have learned the basics of how to draft a process map.

In terms of software, they must have learned the mind-set and visualized the path of the Measure phase.

Send the EN-E-RG-IZ-E summary before the end of the day, encouraging on what has been accomplished and recapitulating the next steps with positive actions: Define tollgate completed (well done!); prepare a first-draft process map.

Typical first-level self-reflective questions:

- What is the objective of the Measure phase?
- What are the expected outcomes and key steps?
- How are you going to visualize how the process works before rushing into collecting data? Why do you need a process map?
- What are the key components to represent in the map?
- What is the best way to ensure the map is accurate and representative of the reality?
- How detailed should the process map be?
- What is the right level of granularity?
- Does the process map fit the project purpose (i.e., help to visualize the CTQs)?

Framed Discussion

LSSC: "Congratulations with the completion of the Define toll-gate! Your project is now officially and formally kicked off; there is no way back in our commitment to make the project a success. So, what's up today?"

B: "Start the Measure phase?"

LSSC: "Indeed! What is the objective of the Measure phase, and which outcomes should be expected?"

B: "Understand how the process works, and gather relevant data that will guide the analysis of the process."

LSSC: "Good! What are you going to do then?"

B: "Start tracking the time we take to answer client requests and execute missions?"

LSSC: "How are you going to do that in practice?"

B: "We record all queries and missions, so I should be able to extract the timestamps from the system."

LSSC: "Across regions and skill sets? Are you confident the different timestamps have the same meaning for all missions?"

B: "Well…indeed, I might need to draw a process map to visualize the process first."

LSSC: "Might be good indeed. What are the key components to represent in the process map?"

B: "The actors, the tasks, the decision points, the flow of tasks, and the interactions between actors."

LSSC: "Right. And how are you going to do it?"

B: "I guess I can start with my knowledge of the process, and then check with each actor involved to enhance the details."

LSSC: "Good plan. What level of detail are you going to look for?"

B: "As detailed as possible?"

LSSC: "Why do you need an advanced level of detail?"

B: "To make sure I capture everything?"

LSSC: "Why is it important to capture everything? Why are you doing a process map?"

B: "To visualize the timeline and measure the gap in the current process from the perspective of the CTQs."

LSSC: "Indeed. So, what is the right level of granularity then?"

B: "OK, I got it: I have to represent what is needed for me to visualize where time is consumed and where delay might be created in the process."

LSSC: "Good. So, in brief, start building a high-level process map from your understanding of the process, enhance it with the information from the various people involved in the process, and continue digging for details until you have a good representation of the metrics linked to your CTQs. It is critical for you to come up with a map representative of the ground reality, staying far, far away from what people think or wish the reality was."

Week 5: Challenging and analyzing the process map

Expect Belts-to-be to come to the session with a first-draft process map.

Work with them on refining the process map, if needed, and linking the map to the CTQs. Challenge the clarity and granularity of the process map until you, the coach, understand it as if you had done it yourself. Try to step back from this specific process and understand how it connects to the overall environment based on other processes you might have worked on before. If it does not make sense with your understanding of the "big picture," there is likely something wrong in the map. By the way, this is a fantastic opportunity for you, as the coach, to learn from the subject-matter expert.

From this stage, different project types, as outlined in Chapter One, are likely to have different deliverables and outcomes.

Quality improvement projects: From the process map, guide Belts-to-be (again using self-reflective questions) on the tasks responsible for poor quality in the process, i.e., where the defects are generated and where time is spent on rework and non-value-added tasks. Teach them how to compute the Cost Of Poor Quality (COPQ) as a transparent, meaningful, and impactful measurement of the poor quality in the process (being the time spent on correcting and inspecting defects, converted into dollars by multiplying by the average fully loaded cost of one FTE (Full Time Equivalent).

Risk reduction projects: Also starting from the process map, guide Belts-to-be with self-reflective questions on where the risk is created in the process. Question them on which tool in the Lean Six Sigma toolbox is available to measure risk, and guide them toward using an FMEA (Failure Modes Effects Analysis) and the RPN (Risk Priority Number) as a measurement of the risk in the current process. Encourage them to organize group's discussions with the key people involved in the process, in order to realistically and neutrally list all the potential failure modes and challenge the outcomes of each task of the process map. For each potential failure mode, the group should come up with a list of impacts, causes, and existing controls; then the group should rank these three components on a one to ten scale. The multiplication of the three components' scores gives an individual RPN per failure mode; the sum of all the individual RPNs is the total RPN of the process. Caution the Belts-to-be to drive the group to properly define, *beforehand*, the ranking scales for severity (or impacts), occurrence (or causes) and detectability (or controls), and agree upon them with the process owner in order to avoid subjective conclusions. Remind them that the final RPN does not matter as a number on its own but as a benchmark to compare project start and end, to evaluate the benefits after the Engineer / Improve phase, and to identify with objective, transparent data the risk concentration areas in the process.

Cycle time reduction projects: From the process map, guide Belts-to-be with self-reflective questions on which tasks are most time-consuming, where waiting times create further delay, and where inventories, backlogs, or any other unsmooth flows create bottlenecks and constraints in the process. Guide them toward using a TAKT time chart as a way to visualize the pain points in the process: get them to identify the blocks of tasks that cannot be parallelized, measure the theoretical time available for each block (total expected cycle time divided by number of "blocks"), and identify the need to measure the time taken by the different blocks of tasks in comparison to the TAKT time. Also guide them toward the need to identify, within each block of tasks, how much time is spent on value-added and non-value-added tasks and waiting, as represented on the TAKT time chart provided in the Measure mind-set section.

Capacity increase projects Beginning with the process map, guide Belts-to-be with self-reflective questions on which tasks are most time-consuming, as well as where most of the volumes creating workload come into the process. Guide them toward the need to conduct a Value Stream Analysis (VSA) working session involving the process owner and the key actors in the process, making them self-aware of where *value* is added in the eyes of the customers, and where it is not. For tasks not having a direct value to the customers, guide them towards challenging the reasons why they are performed: are they process wastes? Regulatory requirements? Are such tasks absolutely needed? Could they be simply stopped? Then, get Belts-to-be to identify the need for measuring the volumes of process inputs, as reducing volumes of manual interventions could tremendously help to increase the capacity of the process.

From there, move to the next steps and analyze the expected challenges. Get Belts-to-be to identify the need to collect data in order to provide factual, non-challengeable conclusions on how big the problem is. Guide them toward the need to prepare a data collection plan before collecting the data. Belts-to-be should then walk out of the session with the mission to prepare the data collection plan and collect data. Caution them of the difficulty of collecting data, but be clear that there is no alternative option: Lean Six Sigma is a data-driven methodology.

At the end of the session, in matters of hardware, Belts-to-be must have learned how to map a process, which tools to use to measure the process in line with the CTQs (COPQ for quality, FMEA for risk, and TAKT time and VSA for time and capacity), and how important it is to prepare a data collection plan.

In terms of software, they must have learned the takeaways of process mapping (used to visualize the process for robust analysis rather than to document it), the need to establish connections between the data to be collected and the project objectives before collecting it, and the importance of collecting adapted and non-challengeable data for proper decision making. Too many non-experts believe that Lean Six Sigma project leaders collect data because it "looks good." At this stage, Belts-to-be must walk away from this idea and be convinced that Lean Six Sigma is called "data-driven methodology" for a good reason.

Send the EN-E-RG-IZ-E summary before the end of the day, encouraging on what has been accomplished and recapitulating the next steps with positive actions: refine the process map if needed, prepare the data collection plan, and collect data.

Typical first-level self-reflective questions to be asked by the coach and meaningfully answered by the Belt-to-be (in the language of the business):

- Where are the defects, risks, time lags, or workload created in the process?
- Where is the cost of poor quality generated in the process (rework, corrections, inspection tasks)?
- Where are the defects and failure modes arising in the process?
- Are waiting times, bottlenecks, constraints, and inventories visualized in the flow?
- What is the output of the process expected by the customer?
- What are the "value-added" versus "non-value-added" tasks?
- How much time is spent creating value versus time lost due to poor quality and waiting?
- From the visualization of the flow, which data should be collected to better understand the process, in line with the project objectives?

This coaching discussion will highly depend on the process map itself. Therefore, the *Framed Discussion* is omitted here.

Week 6: Data collection plan, operational definition, Measurement system analysis

Expect Belts-to-be to come to the session with a data collection plan draft and potentially some data they managed to collect since the last session.

Work with them on reviewing the data collection plan, especially the operational definition and sample size. Remind them of the risk of lack of reproducibility and repeatability in data collection. Challenge them on the robustness of the data collection plan. For Black Belts' development, emphasize the need to run a proper MSA (Measurement System Analysis) with attribute agreement analysis for discrete data (i.e. with a finite number of possible values: 1, 2, 3, 4, 5...) and Gage R&R – a measurement system analysis technique aiming at testing the reproducibility and repeatability of the collected data – for continuous data (i.e. data that can take any value within a range). Then, analyze with them the challenges of collecting data. Question them on difficulties potentially faced and how to walk around them. If they have already collected some data, work with them on understanding the data collected and what is learned from it and which new questions might arise.

Then, move to the next steps and analyze the challenges to expect. Guide them with self-reflective questions on how to link the data to CTQs and project objectives. Challenge them on whether the data collected or planned to be collected is useful for measuring the gap between the current situation and the target expected end state. Is the project progressing as it concerns understanding the current process performance (i.e., how the process *works*)?

At this point of time, Belts-to-be should have gained a fair understanding of the process and its current performance. It might be a good time to ask whether quick wins could be identified: Prepare Belts-to-be to identify potential wastes in the process; Question them about easy, cheap, reversible changes that might immediately improve the process and the customer and sponsor satisfaction.

At the end of the session, in regard to hardware, Belts-to-be must have developed an understanding of the data collection plan, data collection, wastes, and quick wins.

In terms of software, they must have learned the importance of collecting the right data ("right" depending on the project objectives), felt the difficulty of collecting data, and be convinced that however difficult it might be, it will have to be done.

Send the EN-E-RG-IZ-E summary before the end of the day, encouraging on what has been accomplished and recapitulating the next steps with positive actions: continue collecting data, interpreting and challenging data collected, and implementing quick wins, if any.

Typical first-level self-reflective questions:

- What are the specific metrics you plan to measure?
- How do you measure risk? Which data do you need to collect?
- How do you measure quality? Which data do you need to collect?
- What is the cost impact of poor quality / rework / risk in the current process?
- Is the data you plan to measure well connected to the CTQs?
- Will the measurement be transparent and non-challengeable?
- Are the operational definitions clear and explicit enough for the person who is going to collect the data to visualize the steps to do it operationally?
- How can you ensure the people who will collect the data precisely understand what they have to collect and understand it in the same way you do?
- If different people collect the data, are they likely to come up with similar data sets? If the same person collects the data several times, will he/she come up with similar data sets?
- Which types of data do you plan to collect (discrete versus continuous)?
- What should be the minimum sample size according to the required level of precision and confidence?

- Is the data set going to be representative of the reality?
- Is there any specific environmental factor to take into consideration that might skew the data?
- Once the data is collected as planned, what do you expect to learn in the process?
- To what extent do you expect the data you plan to collect to help in understanding the current process performance?
- What difficulties can be expected when collecting the data?
- How much time can be given to data collection without threatening project milestones?

This coaching discussion will depend heavily on the process map and the data collected, specific to each situation. Therefore, the *framed discussion* is omitted here.

Week 7: Understanding the data collected and how the process works

Expect Belts-to-be to come to the session with the data collected. It might take more or less time depending on the difficulty and tools available, but in this section, we assume it is completed, as it is a prerequisite for moving forward on proper grounds. Otherwise, revisit Week 6 and emphasize again the absolute necessity of collecting data.

Once data is collected, work with Belts-to-be on understanding it and linking it back to the CTQs. Guide them toward building some pie charts, Pareto charts, or whatever else helps to *visualize and understand* how the process works. Conclude with the measurement of the gaps between current process performance and expected end state, which might, in practice, lead to different outcomes for different types of initiatives.

Quality improvement projects: The outcome of the data collection should be learning the number of defects and the resulting COPQ (cost measured in time or dollars). Get Belts-to-be to compare these measures to the actual target agreed upon in the Define phase: in most projects, defects and poor quality are expected to reach a minimum. Help Belts-to-be use the Defects Per Million of Opportunities (DPMO) or process capability and Sigma level as the measurement of the actual gap between current and expected process performance.

Risk reduction projects: The outcomes of the data collection should be an FMEA (Failure Modes Effects Analysis), with the list of tasks creating most of the risk inherent to the current process, as well as a list of the main causes and impacts. Pareto charts using the RPN on the X-axis can be used to visualize the risk. A pure, statistical process capability cannot be computed here, but Belts-to-be should get the idea of what it is: the ability of the process to meet customer expectations, i.e., minimal risk to be left in the process and, in any case, major risks to be mitigated.

Cycle time reduction projects: The outcomes of the data collection should be the TAKT time chart and an understanding of time taken for non-value-added tasks, waiting times, bottlenecks, and constraints. Get Belts-to-be to compare the total cycle time to the actual target agreed upon in the Define phase, and help them plot the process capability for continuous data and measure the Sigma level—always an exciting moment in a very first Lean Six Sigma journey.

Capacity increase projects: The outcomes of the data collection should be both time analysis (excluding wait times) and volumes of process inputs. A correlation graph (time versus volumes) could be used to visualize the dependency between both. Whether to tackle one, the other, or both depends on each individual project. In any case, at this point of the Lean Six Sigma development, Belts-to-be should be guided toward measuring the gap between current and target process performances and assisted in using process capability analysis with discrete or continuous data as a statistical methodology for measuring this gap.

Then, move to the next steps and analyze the expected challenges. Belts-to-be should be close to the end of the Measure phase, but should also be advised before continuing the journey to take a bit of time to step back and ensure the data and conclusions are meaningful, robust, and clear enough for understanding the problem stated in the Define phase.

At the end of the session, in regard to hardware, Belts-to-be must have learned data collection and process capability.

In terms of software, they must have learned the mind-set and path of the Measure phase—a factual, non-challengeable measurement of the gap between the current process performance and the target state expected by the customers and sponsor.

Send the EN-E-RG-IZ-E summary before the end of the day, encouraging on what has been accomplished and recapitulating the next steps with positive actions: collect more data if necessary, measure the process capability (i.e., ability of the process to meet customer expectations), and step back and understand the meaning of the conclusions in the language of the business environment.

Typical first-level self-reflective questions related to this discussion:

- How do you link the data collected to the CTQs?
- What did you learn from the data collected? What else?
- Does the data confirm your expectations? If not, why, and is it still in line with the business's logic?
- What is the average? What are the variations?
- How far is the current process from customer expectations?
- What is the process capability?
- In view of the actual gap, are the project objectives still achievable and realistic within the committed timeline?
- Do you see some trends in the data?
- Is there any input parameter (X) explaining significant process variations? Can you prove it statistically?
- Is there any interaction between different significant Xs?
- Does the data collected match with your understanding of the process?
- How did you measure the poor quality? Number of defects? Cost?
- How did you measure the process risk?
- How can you be confident the quality/risk measurement is transparent: neither subjective nor challengeable?
- Which chart(s) will you use to help visualize the outputs of the process measurement?

Framed Discussion

In our Case Study #5, the three CTQs are 1) reducing cycle time to provide an answer to clients requests to below three days, 2) improving the process quality by reducing to as close to zero as possible the number of missions not completed as committed to clients, and 3) reducing the risk of inappropriately accepting or rejecting a mission.

LSSC: "Hi! What's up today?"

B: "I managed to collect the data as defined in the data collection plan. I have good data sets regarding time required to answer calls in the different regions and number of missions not completed as committed over the overall missions contracted with each client, and I also filled in the FMEA table. Now, I am lost in the huge amount of data. What should I do?"

LSSC: "Let's decompose the problem CTQ by CTQ. Let's start with the time required to answer calls. What did you learn from the data collected?"

B: "I have too much data. I do not know where to start."

LSSC: "Alright. Maybe let's start with the size of the problem: what is the average time to answer calls, and how much variation do you observe in the sample?"

B: "On average, we provide an answer to our clients within seven days. But it seems to vary a lot across client regions and skill sets required."

LSSC: "Ah, interesting! Not only you have measured the average size of the problem (three to seven: four days), but you have also identified two significant X's explaining variations in the process! Can you tell me more? To what extent do the client location and the skill sets impact answering time? Have you plotted the process capability per region and per skill set?"

B: "Yes. Even though our office is located in Europe, we have clients in three regions: Asia, Europe, and North America. All client requests originating in Europe and Asia are answered within five days, while requests originating in North America are answered within ten days. For all regions, the variations are one to two days."

LSSC: "Good start. Do you conclude the client location is a significant X then?"

B: "It seems obvious, right?"

LSSC: "What does obvious mean?"

B: "Alright, I get it. I will run some hypothesis tests to confirm."

LSSC: "Good. Beyond statistics, is the conclusion in line with your understanding of the process?"

B: "Yes, it makes sense, as for many US-based requests sent after European working hours, we only answer on the next day and get delayed each time we need to interact with the clients."

LSSC: "Very good! How about the skill sets?"

B: "Our company categorizes the skill sets into three groups: advisory-, audit-, and tax-related matters. Feedback to clients on audit requests are given in three days on average, tax in five days, and advisory in eleven days. And most of our missions are advisory related."

LSSC: "Alright. Can you prove the skill set is a significant X then? Any reason why it is so? Does it make any sense to you?"

B: "I will run the hypothesis tests here as well. I am not fully confident I understand why, though. I will need to speak to the representatives of each sector."

LSSC: "OK. Do you see any interactions between regions and skill sets?"

B: "I have not checked. That's something I can further investigate."

LSSC: "Any other input parameters that seem to be responsible for variations?"

B: "Not yet. I am collecting more data from the advisory group to find out if the number of resources available in the company is sized in line with the number of client requests received. Shortage of resources in this group might explain why their performance is not as good as in the other groups."

LSSC: "Good. What else? Could the answer provided to the client (yes or no) have an impact on the timeliness to answer?"

B: "I do not know. I will find out."

LSSC: "OK. So, regarding timeliness in providing answers to clients, you need to validate statistically whether region and skill sets are significant Xs, understand the variations across different skill set groups (especially advisory), validate whether skill sets and regions are independent, and find out whether accepting or rejecting the mission impacts the timeliness of an answer. How about the CTQ related to quality, i.e., the number of missions not completed as committed?"

B: "Here again, I have a lot of data, and I do not know where to start."

LSSC: "Have you identified any significant X yet?"

B: "No. With what we just discussed, I will try to find out whether the same Xs (region and skill set) have an impact and validate the assumptions with hypothesis tests."

LSSC: "Yes, that makes sense. What else?"

B: "Mmm...maybe I could look at how late the defective missions are?"

LSSC: "That would be a good idea. What else?"

B: "Let me start with this first and find out more investigation areas from the skill set groups' team leaders."

LSSC: "Good idea. Let's speak about your third CTQ then: reducing the process risk. How did you measure it?"

B: "I filled in the FMEA with the different people involved and now have the total RPN, but it does not mean much to me..."

LSSC: "Indeed, the RPN itself is not what matters most. Before we go into the details, can you explain to me how you ranked the different severity, occurrence, and detection factors?"

B: "I talked to all the different people and ranked each one compared to each other based on the overall understanding of the process."

LSSC: "The relative ranking is a good point. But how do you make sure the ranking is not biased by impressions and subjectivity?"

B: "Ah, I recall now. I have to work on the ranking scales separately first, and then make the ranks match with the factors in the table."

LSSC: "Yes. How do you rank the severity factors?"

B: "I could look back at the voice of the customers: 1 would match with what 'good' looks like in their eyes, 10 with the worst scenarios, and I could gradually define the area between the different levels of satisfaction?"

LSSC: "Indeed. The severity scale is driven by the customers. How about the occurrence scale?"

B: "This one is easy: I will look at the actual number of instances: 1 when it never happens, 10 when it happens several times daily, and I will gradually define the different levels of likelihood in between."

LSSC: "Great. How about the detection?"

B: "Similarly: 1 when a control is in place to systematically detect the failure mode, 10 if there is no control, and gradual definition of detections modes in between."

LSSC: "Great. It is very important to have such transparent ranking scales, in line with the business meaning of your process, to avoid a subjective measurement of the risk and to transparently explain how you come up with the numbers to be used to make decisions later on. What to do then?"

B: "Then I need to rank the inputs in the FMEA from highest to lowest RPN, which will give me the most critical failure modes and riskiest process steps."

LSSC: "Good. What to do then?"

B: "List the failure modes that trigger 80 percent of the RPN and prevent the failure modes from happening, which will reduce the risk."

LSSC: "Indeed. How do you proceed for each critical failure mode?"

B: "I do not remember. Can you remind me?"

LSSC: "Sure. First, try to address the causes; if the causes can be eradicated, the failure modes will disappear. If and only if nothing can be done about the causes, look at reducing the severity of the impact. And if and only if that is not possible either, let's look at adding controls in the process. Anyway, we are already stepping into the next phase here. For now, in the Measure phase, we are looking at facts: I would suggest building Pareto charts using the RPN, plotting the most critical failure modes and the most critical causes. We can then see the outcomes and move into the analysis."

B: "Alright. I will do that."

LSSC: "Good. So, in brief, dig further into the data related to the timeliness of answering clients, as we said, find out significant Xs for the defective missions, review the ranks in the FMEA to make them neutral, and build the Pareto charts showing the most critical failure modes and their causes. Once you have consolidated the data, step back and comment on it in the eyes of the *business*. It is critical to gather all this data in a very factual and visual manner, as data is going to drive decisions in the next phases: facts should not be challengeable."

Week 8: Wrap-up of the Measure phase

Expect Belts-to-be to come to the session with the outcomes of the Measure phase: (1) visualization of the process (process map); (2) understanding of the current process performance (data collection plan, graphs representing the current process performance: pie charts, Pareto charts, etc.); (3) measurement of the gap between current and target processes (using the appropriate representation depending on the project type, as suggested in the section on the Measure mind-set on pages 69 to 72).

Work with Belts-to-be on internalizing the above three factual outcomes of the Measure phase and ask whether they are worth being presented to the sponsor at this point of time or should be presented with the outcomes of the Analyze phase (i.e., the root causes of the problem). My view here is that most sponsors, when seeing only facts, are likely to ask, "so what?" and will be much more interested in getting the root causes together. However, some sponsors who are closer to the process itself like numbers and are willing to see them as soon as possible. As the coach, discuss this with Belts-to-be and agree on what best suits the stakeholders and the context.

Then, move to the next steps and analyze the challenges to expect: prepare the Measure tollgate, if such an option is chosen, and start the Analyze phase. In any case, whether the Measure tollgate is presented now or combined with the Analyze tollgate, I strongly recommended that you help Belts-to-be prepare what should be presented to a sponsor regarding the Measure phase without waiting. It saves time for the next tollgate, as it is always easier and faster to prepare a presentation when the data and outcomes are still "fresh" in people minds. From a learning standpoint, it also helps to summarize and visualize the outcomes for Belts-to-be.

At the end of the session, in matters of hardware, Belts-to-be must have learned and interiorized the key outcomes of the Measure phase.

In terms of software, they must have learned to review data and put it back into the business context, prepare a presentation at the end of the Measure phase, and understand sponsor expectations regarding deliverables and updates.

Send the EN-E-RG-IZ-E summary before the end of the day, encouraging on what has been accomplished and recapitulating the next steps with positive actions: prepare the slides summarizing the conclusions and outcomes of the Measure phase (facts!); start the Analyze phase.

Typical first-level self-reflective questions related to this discussion:

- What is the learning from each tool?
- Which factual conclusion can be drawn from each step?
- Is the problem stated in the Define phase decomposed and measured in line with the CTQs?
- Which chart(s) best allow for visualization of the current process performance?
- Which additional comment/conclusion is worth highlighting on top of the charts?
- How could the cost impact of poor quality and risk be measured?
- Are all these results worth presenting in a Tollgate? Or should they be combined with the conclusions of the Analyze phase?
- Are the stakeholders interested in seeing the facts and numbers, or do you expect them to be more excited by the root causes and the explanations of the problem?

Framed Discussion

LSSC: "Hi! What's up today?"

B: "I have collected further data, as discussed last week, and consolidated the outcomes of the Measure phase. Let's look at the contents."

LSSC: "Great plan! Tell me more."

B: "I have the process map, the data collection plan, and the different data sets and their conclusions."

LSSC: "Good. Do you want to present all these results in a tollgate, or do you prefer to combine with the Analyze phase?"

B: "What do you recommend?"

LSSC: "Do you think the stakeholders are interested in seeing the facts and numbers, or do you expect them to be more excited by the root causes and the explanations of the problem?"

B: "These guys are usually busy: I think they would rather want to combine and go straight to the conclusive explanations."

LSSC: "OK. So, let's not organize a formal meeting now, but let's still prepare what you would present if you had one. That will help you to refine the data and make everything ready for the Measure and Analyze tollgate. Starting with the process map, what would you present?"

B: "Should I show the detailed map?"

LSSC: "Does the map help you illustrate any noticeable fact to explain the problem?"

B: "Well, it shows the timeline and the poor quality…"

LSSC: "So, why not show a high-level map, highlighting the tasks accountable for poor quality, as well as the overall timeline?"

B: "Good idea. I can circle in red all the rework and corrections, show the wait times, and show the actual timeline versus the expected three days."

LSSC: "Indeed. How could you better represent the gap between the current performance and the expected three days?"

B: "I could show the process capability charts?"

LSSC: "Indeed, that is one way. Another option would be to present a TAKT time chart: showing the different blocks of tasks by column on the X-axis and showing within each column (with a color code for example) how much time is spent on value-added tasks, rework, investigations, and waiting, with time plotted on the Y-axis. That would give you an overall picture of the time repartition, and the process capability charts per region and skill set would help to show the next level of detail. Decompose the message problem by problem, or CTQ by CTQ: one page for the map, one page for timeliness, one page for quality. On each page, what else is critical to add to the illustrative maps and charts?"

B: "Comments, I guess?"

LSSC: "Yes, highlight the top three, four, or five key learning points from each graph in a very factual form. Within these comments, why not provide an estimate of the actual cost (in dollars) of poor quality and risk in the process?"

B: "That would be good, but how to do that?"

LSSC: "Once you have measured how much time is spent on such tasks, multiply by the average fully loaded cost of one man hour. This will give a good proxy and a sense of the financial benefits at stake."

B: "OK."

LSSC: "So, that is for process map, time analysis and quality. How about risk?"

B: "I do not think I want to present the details of the FMEA."

LSSC: "I agree. How can you help the audience visualize where the risk comes from in the process?"

B: "I could use the Pareto charts built using the RPN."

LSSC: "Good. So, indeed, you have another page for the last CTQ, with the Pareto charts and conclusive yet factual comments on where the risk of not being able to complete the missions as committed sits in the current process. Anything else?"

B: "Should I include the data collection plan?"

LSSC: "Why did you use a data collection plan, and do you think it is interesting to the stakeholders?"

B: "I did it to make the measurement robust and transparent. Indeed, not very useful for drawing conclusions on how the process performs."

LSSC: "Great. So, in brief, the Measure phase is made of the process map on which the COPQ is highlighted, 1 page per CTQ (timeliness, quality, risk), with each page including a chart to visualize the current process performance and a few bullet points drawing factual conclusions on the size of the problem. Such factual and non-challengeable conclusions are critical to moving forward in your project."

Analyze

If you can't explain it simply, you do not understand it well enough.

—Albert Einstein

The Analyze mind-set

The understanding that should be built into the Belt-to-be brain at this stage is that the Analyze phase aims at identifying the root causes of specific problems (problem or gap, as measured in the Measure phase). Then comes the question of what "root" means, how to ensure when the "roots" are really found, and when you can stop digging further down. Some important characteristics of good "root causes" can be highlighted from that moment to Belts-to-be: they are simple and self-explanatory and turn problems into solutions. To put it into Einstein's words: *"It should be possible to explain the laws of physics to a barmaid."* The same applies to a business challenge after it is transformed by the "Define, Measure, Analyze" process: the stakeholders should then be able to truly, simply and transparently *understand* the problem to the point that they should be able to explain the problem in their own words, objective of Pillar Two of the Lean Six Sigma mind-set.

Regarding the exhaustiveness of the root causes, a good question to ask is whether Belts-to-be are confident the problem (as stated in the Define phase) will be resolved if all the root causes are addressed. To quote Einstein again: "Knowledge of what is does not necessarily open the door of what should be." We are not talking about providing solutions yet. Guide Belts-to-be to think in the ideal world where solutions to all the root causes will be found later on: Are they ready to sign off that resolving all the root causes will eventually allow them to reach the expected end state? I have found this checkpoint very helpful in practically knowing when to stop searching and digging for root causes.

Template: the conclusions of the Analyze phase
Completing the Analyze phase should lead to filling in the following table:

Problem statements	Root causes	Ref	Impact on CTQ1	Impact on CTQ2	Impact on CTQ3	...
Problem 1 E.g.: re-work rate = 45%	Root cause 1	RC1				
	Root cause 2	RC2				
	Root cause 3	RC3				
Problem 2 E.g.: cycle time beyond target by 4 hours	Root cause 4	RC4				
	Root cause 5	RC5				
	Root cause 6	RC6				
	Root cause 7	RC7				
...	...					
		Total	xxx	xxx	xxx	...

Week 9: Introduction to the Analyze phase

Expect Belts-to-be to come to the session with the slides recapitulating the Measure phase.

Introduce the Analyze phase: Start by questioning Belts-to-be on the objectives and expected outcomes, developing this reflex to associate "Analyze" with "root causes."

Once the Analyze mind-set is introduced, work with Belts-to-be on how to find those root causes. From the factual gaps summarized in the conclusions of the Measure phase, start asking why. Get Belts-to-be to truly understand and interiorize the principle of asking why again, and again. A good way to introduce the main causes of the problems (not the roots yet) and get started in the exercise of continuously asking "Why?" is to guide Belts-to-be to use an FMEA (Failure Modes Effects Analysis). Then, using a Pareto chart built on the RPN by causes helps to identify the main area of investigations, from where Belts-to-be can build the Five Why's analysis. They should walk out of this session with the mission of using an FMEA to identify the main causes having the biggest impact on the problems existing in the process and should start the Five Why's (or Fishbone) analysis from there. The challenge they should be prepared for is to tirelessly ask why until the root causes have been found.

At the end of the session, in matters of hardware, Belts-to-be must have learned the basic principles of FMEA (Failure Modes Effects Analysis) and the Five Why's (Fishbone).

In terms of software, they must have learned the essence of the Analyze phase and the difficulties to expect when formulating a strong, comprehensive *understanding* of the process.

Send the EN-E-RG-IZ-E summary before the end of the day, encouraging on what has been accomplished and recapitulating the next steps with positive actions: use an FMEA to assess the main causes of the problem in the process; start the Five Why's analysis.

Typical first-level self-reflective questions related to this discussion:

- What is the objective of the Analyze phase?
- What are the expected outcomes and key steps?
- What is the best way to find the root causes of the problem?
- What is critical to the success of the root causes analysis?
- When do you stop asking "Why?"

Framed Discussion

LSSC: "Congratulations on the Measure phase! What's up today?"

B: "Starting the Analyze phase. I now know what the problem is and how big it is. What should I do next?"

LSSC: "Yes. What is the objective of the Analyze phase, and which outcomes should be expected?"

B: "Recalling from the training…listing and ranking the root causes of the problem. The tools available are Fishbone and Five Why's analysis."

LSSC: "Yes. How are you going to proceed?"

B: "Well, the key problems are listed from the Measure phase, so I could do one Five Why's analysis for each problem."

LSSC: "Good. What is critical to the success of such analysis?"

B: "It has to come from the people performing the process. OK, I will organize the meeting and get a consensual understanding of the root causes of the problem."

LSSC: "Great. So, in brief, list the specific problems coming out of the Measure phase, and ask 'Why?' as many times as you need, i.e., until you reach the root causes of the problems. Remember that asking 'Why?' is going to help turn problems into solutions, turn opponents into change partners, and help identify real problems, as opposed to impressions of problems. It is critical to dig as far as you need with the people involved in the process to avoid a high resistance to change later on in the Engineer / Improve phase."

Week 10: Root causes analysis

Expect Belts-to-be to come to the session with drafts of FMEA (Failure Modes Effects Analysis) and Five Why's. Work with them on building Pareto charts from the FMEA, hence identifying the main causes creating the pain in the process. Challenge the Five Why's analysis, getting them to go deeper and deeper.

Then, move to the next steps and analyze the expected challenges. Explain the importance of the Five Why's analysis in building consensus around where the problem really is. Encourage them to conduct a working session with the process owner and key actors in the process to go further and deeper in the root causes analysis. Guide them toward understanding the importance of prioritizing the different root causes in order to eventually solve the problem effectively and efficiently with minimal effort. Get them to go back to collect more data if the problem is not fully and clearly explained with the data collected in the first round of measurement.

For Black Belt journeys, encourage the use of statistical analysis (hypothesis testing) to validate and rank the root causes from highest to lowest impact on the problem stated in the Define phase.

At the end of the session, in matters of hardware, Belts-to-be must have learned how to practically use FMEA and Five Why's to identify the root causes of the problem raised in the Define phase.

In terms of software, they must have learned the power of asking "Why?" in matters of change management: turning problems into opportunities, changing opponents into change partners, and identifying where the real problems are (as opposed to impressions of a problem). They should also be convinced of the power of asking "Why?" and "What if…?" to constantly challenge a process, anytime, and be keen to propose continuous improvements—even beyond any Lean Six Sigma dedicated initiative.

Send the EN-E-RG-IZ-E summary before the end of the day, encouraging on what has been accomplished and recapitulating the next steps with positive actions: finalize the root causes analysis, and rank the different root causes by their impact on the problem stated in the Define phase.

Week 11: Going further and deeper into the root causes

Expect the Belts-to-be to come to the session with the root causes analysis and an assessment of the impact of each root cause on the problem stated in the Define phase. Work with them on wording these root causes as *problem statements*: the list of simply articulated problems to be resolved in order to resolve the problem stated in the Define phase. Guide them to measure the impact of each problem statement on the overall problem, going back to the data collected to provide factual numbers when measuring the impacts. Challenge them on the numbers and on their confidence that the list of problem statements does explain the overall problem.

Then, move to the next steps and analyze the challenges to expect: preparing the Measure & Analyze tollgate (or Analyze only if Measure has been presented earlier) and being ready to answer the questions the stakeholders are likely to ask.

At the end of the session, in matters of hardware, Belts-to-be must have learned how to write problem statements and objectively rank them by their impact on the overall problem stated in the Define phase.

In terms of software, they must have learned the outcome of the Analyze phase: a list of self-explanatory, simply articulated problem statements and a measurement of their impacts on each CTQ as a way to define priorities to effectively resolve the overall problem.

Send the EN-E-RG-IZ-E summary before the end of the day, encouraging on what has been accomplished and recapitulating the next steps with positive actions: finalize the list of problem statements, rank the individual problem statements by their impact on the overall problem, and start preparing the document to be presented in the Measure & Analyze tollgate.

The questions related to Week 10 and 11 discussions are grouped, as these sessions are likely to raise back-and-forth questions until all answers are provided by Belts-to-be: As answers are unlikely to be deep enough on the first trial, two weeks are dedicated to this critical step of the Lean Six Sigma development journey.

Typical first-level self-reflective questions to be answered by Belts-to-be:

- Will the problem be resolved if we can manage to address all the so-called 'root causes'?
- Have the causes (or significant Xs) been validated graphically (pie charts, Pareto charts, etc.) and / or statistically (hypothesis testing)?
- How much of the problem is explained by each root cause?
- What if the entire problem is not explained? Is the gap acceptable (i.e., within customer specification limits)?
- Should we go back to collecting more data to finalize the root causes analysis? Is there a need to dig further down to the roots?
- What are the root causes critical to address?
- Which one should be addressed first? And then? And then?
- What are the key simply articulated problems concluding the Analyze phase?
- If these problems are all resolved, will the gap (measured in the Measure phase) be closed in line with the project's objectives?
- If these problems are all resolved, should further benefits in addition to the ones anticipated in the Define phase be expected? (*Tip: Think about costs, customer satisfaction, risk/safety/control, quality, process capacity, and process timeliness.*)

The contents of these coaching discussions will highly depend on the problems and the root causes Belts-to-be come up with, specific to each situation. Therefore, the *framed discussion* is omitted.

Week 12: Preparation of the Measure & Analyze tollgate

Expect Belts-to-be to come to the session with a draft document of the Measure & Analyze tollgate. Work with them on preparing the slides and articulating the story line. Guide them toward starting with a quick reminder of the last tollgate: the key success factors, or CTQs (assuming the Measure & Analyze tollgates are combined). Then guide them to present the factual analysis of the Measure phase: from where in the process the problem comes and how big it is compared to the expected end state. If the problem is a combination of quality, risk, time, and/or capacity, get them to decompose the "message" (with one slide per objective, for example). Get them to end the *story* with the list of problem statements, root causes, and their individual impact on each CTQ: a concise summary can be presented as proposed in the table concluding the section on the Analyze mindset on page 94.

Finish with an opening on the next steps: plans to design solutions to the list of simple problems concluding the Analyze phase (yet without providing the solutions themselves), highlighting the potential need to on-board additional resources to design the solutions for which the support of the sponsor might be required.

Then, analyze the challenges to expect from the stakeholders: Which questions are likely to be asked? What to answer? Can appendices to the document help to answer difficult questions? Should any actor in the process attend the meeting to help answer some challenging questions or contribute to the credibility of the analysis?

At the end of the session, in matters of hardware, Belts-to-be must have interiorized the tools and outcomes of the Measure & Analyze phases.

In terms of software, they must have learned to prepare a Measure & Analyze tollgate meeting and articulate its story line as well as anticipate difficult questions likely to arise from stakeholders, who must be convinced of the strength and robustness of the conclusions.

Send the EN-E-RG-IZ-E summary before the end of the day, encouraging on what has been accomplished and recapitulating the next steps with positive actions: schedule the Measure & Analyze tollgate, finalize the preparation of the document, and prepare the story line.

Typical first-level self-reflective questions related to this discussion:

- What is the objective of the meeting?
- What is expected from the audience?
- What is the agenda?
- Is the audience interested in the working paths to the root causes? Or are the people willing to see only the final explanation of the problem? Or anything in between?
- Are the conclusions coming out of the Measure phase factual and non-debatable?
- Are the conclusions of the Analyze phase simply articulated so that anyone in the audience can easily understand, to the extent people could explain the problems in their own words?
- Is the problem simply but rigorously explained and quantified?
- Are the priorities clearly set?

Framed Discussion

LSSC: "Hi! What's up today?"

B: "I have prepared a draft of the document to be presented in the Measure & Analyze tollgate. Let's review it together?"

LSSC: "Sure. Tell me more."

B: "We had worked on the conclusions of the Measure phase a few weeks ago, so I already have everything: process map, and one page per CTQ with charts and factual comments. Then, I have added one page per Fishbone (one per CTQ) and highlighted the root causes on each."

LSSC: "Alright. Before going into the contents, what is the objective of the meeting? What do you expect from the stakeholders, and what is the agenda?"

B: "Ah, yes. The objective is to conclude the Measure and Analyze phases, getting the sign-off of the sponsor to move to Engineer / Improve. Agenda: process map and COPQ highlighted, factual measurement of the problem CTQ by CTQ, root causes."

LSSC: "Great! Then, indeed, we have already prepared the contents from the Measure phase. How about the root causes?"

B: "I intended to present the Fishbone diagrams and highlight the root causes from there. What do you think?"

LSSC: "It is an option. However, do you consider the Fishbone diagrams conclusive or working documents?"

B: "A little bit of both: the working paths to the root causes, as well as the conclusions at the roots."

LSSC: "Indeed. Do you think the working paths to the root matter to the stakeholders?"

B: "They care mainly about the conclusions but might ask how to get there."

LSSC: "Indeed. So, why not present the conclusions only, as a list of the simply articulated problems from highest to lowest priority, together with the impact of each problem on each CTQ?"

B: "Good. That would help me to consolidate everything into one page and one message. But what if I am asked how I reached such conclusions?"

LSSC: "Why not add the Fishbone diagrams in the Appendix then? You can refer to it if questions come, i.e., only if someone is interested."

B: "Great, I will prepare this summary page of the Analyze phase: one table listing the root causes from highest to lowest importance on the overall problem and their impacts on each CTQ."

LSSC: "Good. So, in brief, prepare the summary of the Analyze phase, and, most importantly, prepare the story line from the beginning of the Measure phase to the conclusions of the Analyze phase. It is critical to present the outcomes as facts, naturally driving you to explain the problem in a logical, quantified manner."

Week 13: Debrief on the Measure & Analyze tollgate

Expect Belts-to-be to come to the session after sending the minutes of the Measure & Analyze tollgate to the stakeholders.

Debrief them on the tollgate and the Measure & Analyze phases as the Second Pillar of the Lean Six Sigma mind-set.

Move on to the Engineer / Improve phase.

Engineer / Improve

A pessimist sees the difficulty in every opportunity; an optimist sees the opportunity in every difficulty.
— *Winston Churchill*

The Engineer / Improve mind-set

The Engineer / Improve phase aims at providing solutions to the *root causes* of the problem, not to its symptoms. But the trick is that the effectiveness of the improvement should be measured by the transformation of the *symptoms*. Let's illustrate the concept on Sally's disease, as discussed in Chapter Two: the solution (antibiotic) is designed from the root cause (bacteria), but its effectiveness is measured by how much of the symptoms disappear (Sally gets better: fever and stomach pain disappear). Engineering or Improving is a difficult process that requires a fair bit of optimism and positive thinking. *"Pessimism never won any battle,"* said Eisenhower. Belts-to-be will have to be prepared to never run out of optimism in the Improve phase in order to win the battle.

This phase starts with generating ideas to address the specific problem statements listed at the end of the Analyze phase—as much and as many as possible—and it must be done as a group to avoid strong resistance to change later on. As Steve Jobs said: *"Things don't have to change the world to be important."* As long as the suggested changes help to address those root causes, they are good ideas to bring forward.

Then, the new process must be *practically* designed into an end-to-end flow by consolidating and connecting many individual ideas. Belts-to-be must be prepared for the likelihood of facing the greatest challenges of the project at this stage, simply because changing is diffi-cult. Engineer / Improve is likely to consist of trials, failures, and trials again, and belts-to-be should be aware of this going into this phase. *"A person who never made a mistake never tried anything,"* said Albert Einstein. The miraculous solution is unlikely to be standing around the corner, waiting to be picked up. A full-scale process improvement initiative would not have been necessary if that were the case.

Finally, the new process must be implemented. This level of ac-complishment will require great effort. To put it into English histo-rian Thomas Fuller's words, *"One that would have the fruit must climb the tree."* The reward is even sweeter when the journey has been chal-lenging. Be patient and perseverant in making the change real and effective, and everyone around you will be impressed by the results.

Template: the conclusions of the Engineer / Improve phase
Completing the Engineer / Improve phase should lead to filling in the following table and chart and referencing the CTQs as stated in the Define phase and the root causes and impacts as stated in the Measure & Analyze phases:

Root causes	Ref	Proposed Improvement	Dependencies (systems, teams...)	Cost (implementation effort)	Impact on CTQ1	Impact on CTQ2	Impact on CTQ3	...
Root cause 1	RC1-1							
	RC1-2							
Root cause 2	RC2-1							
	RC2-2							
	RC2-3							
Root cause 3	RC3-1							
	RC3-2							
...	...							
Total					XXX	XXX	XXX	...

Week 13 (cont'd): Introduction to the Engineer / Improve phase

Introduce the Engineer / Improve phase and analyze the expected challenges. Question Belts-to-be on the objectives and expected outcomes in line with the specific Lean Six Sigma initiative being run. Remind them of the *mind-set* of the Engineer / Improve phase.

Once the Engineer / Improve mind-set is introduced, work with Belts-to-be on how to start generating ideas to solve the root causes (problem statements, outcomes of the Analyze phase). Caution them that solutions to the *root causes* of the problem must be found, rather than solutions to the problem itself. Guide them toward identifying the method they want to use to generate solutions, cautioning them again that ideas must be generated in groups (as the idea of a group is always greater than the sum of individual ideas, and it helps to build consensus around the change). If they do not know how to proceed, guide them toward conducting some brainstorming working sessions with some people to be chosen appropriately: engaging the people involved in the daily activities, and making those people feel part of the team building the new process is critical from this stage, in order to prevent resistance to change when implementing the new process later on.

Analyze the challenges to be expected in a brainstorming meeting. Help Belts-to-be organize the brainstorming (structured around the problem statements, or root causes), but let them facilitate it, as it is key for a Lean Six Sigma expert to acquire such skills. Highlight the key outcomes they should come up with so that they do not lose sight of what to deliver and let the working session drag out of control.

At the end of the session, in matters of hardware, Belts-to-be must have learned what a brainstorming meeting aims at delivering and how to prepare it.

In terms of software, they must have learned the Engineer / Improve mind-set and key deliverable (new process designed and implemented).

Send the EN-E-RG-IZ-E summary before the end of the day, encouraging on what has been accomplished and recapitulating the next steps with positive actions: congratulate them on the Measure & Analyze tollgate, prepare the brainstorming meetings, and organize and facilitate the brainstorming meetings, eventually coming up with ideas to improve the process.

Typical first-level self-reflective questions:

- What is the objective of the Engineer / Improve phase?
- What are the expected outcomes and key steps?
- How do you generate ideas that make a real change?
- How do you generate ideas that will address the root causes and not just patch the symptoms?
- Who should be involved in the design of the target process?
- How do you get people performing the daily tasks to feel involved and concerned by the design of the new process?
- How do you encourage people to think "out-of-the-box"?
- How do you build ideas as groups?
- How do you manage conflicting ideas in a group discussion?
- How do you build stronger, more powerful ideas from initial thoughts?

The contents of this coaching discussion will be highly dependent upon the problems and the root causes the Belt-to-be has come up with, specific to each situation. Therefore, the *framed discussion* is omitted.

Week 14: Unitary improvements and design of the target process

Expect Belts-to-be to come to the session with a list of ideas for improving the process, targeted toward addressing the root causes of the problem. Work with them on linking each idea to how much of each root cause it helps to address. Challenge them to think through to the end of each idea, elaborating on solutions proposed in the brainstorming meetings. Guide them toward assessing the cost of implementing the changes and using a solution selection matrix to benchmark and compare the relevance of each proposed solution. Get them to keep only what is practical and brings tangible benefits, even though it might be frustrating to drop some ideas that looked good at first sight.

Then, move to the next steps and analyze the expected challenges. Guide them toward designing the new process while retaining the practical and relevant solutions and using an FMEA (Failure Modes Effects Analysis) to assess the risk in the new process. Also suggest using some Poke Yoke (mistake proofing) tips and tools to reduce the likelihood of defects coming out of the process—or at least increase the likelihood of spotting them before they impact the customers or the process. Why not use a QFD (Quality Function Deployment) as a way to design the new process from the voice of the customer fundamental pillars? Indeed, a QFD is a technique helping to weight the relationships between the proposed solutions and the voice of the customer; so a QFD is an efficient tool to design the solution meeting customers' requirements at best.

At the end of the session, in matters of hardware, Belts-to-be must have learned to assess cost versus benefits, when and how to use a Solution Selection Matrix, and how to use an FMEA to assess the risk in a process before its implementation.

In terms of software, they must have learned the difference between generating ideas (thinking "out-of the-box") and making weighted decisions to keep only the practical improvements that do make a difference.

Send the EN-E-RG-IZ-E summary before the end of the day, encouraging on what has been accomplished and recapitulating the next steps with positive actions: short-list the solutions that do help to practically and effectively address the root causes, design the new process, and assess the risks in the new process.

Typical first-level self-reflective questions:

- Are all root causes addressed by the proposals?
- Which portion of each root cause is addressed by each recommendation?
- What is the quantified impact of each suggestion on each CTQ?
- Are all the suggestions practical?
- Should some of the suggestions be dropped as not possible to implement in the current environment? If yes, how do you select the best? What are the criteria for selecting "good" solutions?
- Should anyone in particular be on-boarded to drive the implementation of some suggestions?
- Do the recommendations require some budget for system repair or enhancement, team reorganization, etc.? If yes, who would feel the greatest benefits and be willing to sponsor?
- What is the impact on the problem versus the effort required to implement the individual changes?
- Are some suggestions conflicting? If yes, how do you help stakeholders make the right decisions and select the best?
- What solutions are critical to implement for having the greatest impact on resolving the problem?

The contents of this coaching discussion will be highly dependent upon the proposals made by the teams to improve the process, specific to each situation. Therefore, the *framed discussion* is omitted.

Week 15: From a dense list of unitary suggestions to a practical target process flow

Expect Belts-to-be to come to the session with a target process map and an FMEA (Failure Modes Effects Analysis) measuring the risk in the new process. Work with them on assessing whether the new process does resolve the problem, as stated in the Define phase, or, in other words, has the expected impact on the symptoms of the problem. Challenge them on potential risks created in the new process and the potential need to add controls to mitigate those risks.

Then, move to the next steps and analyze the challenges to expect. If the new process does not yet meet sponsor and customer expectations (i.e., does not positively answer the CTQs checklist), question them on how to fill in the remaining gaps to reach the target—the answer is likely to be found from the root causes analysis. Once the process looks robust and risk-free and is meeting the target, it should be validated by the stakeholders and tested. Hence the Engineer / Improve tollgate should come at this point to validate the design, even though the Engineer / Improve phase is not completed (as the new process has not yet been implemented). Presenting the tollgate at this stage also opens the door to potential ideas the sponsor and other stakeholders not involved in the design itself might have for enriching the new process.

At the end of the session, in matters of hardware, Belts-to-be must have learned to design the target process (including additional controls if needed) and to objectively assess whether it addresses the business problem.

In terms of software, they must have learned to self-assess the relevance of the deliverables by establishing and challenging the connections between CTQs, root causes, and the answer provided to resolve the business problem.

Send the EN-E-RG-IZ-E summary before the end of the day, encouraging on what has been accomplished and recapitulating the next steps with positive actions: tune the target process and risk assessment if needed, identify further improvements if objectives are not met, and start preparing the document to be presented in the next tollgate.

Typical first-level self-reflective questions:

- How do the individual changes fit into a target process flow?
- What is the estimated target performance of the overall process?
- Will the overall gap between current and target performances be closed if all solutions are implemented? If not, what alternative/additional improvements can be made?
- Will the clients be satisfied by the new process performance?
- Are some new risks potentially created in the target process?
- Is there a need to define new controls or to make the process more robust to avoid risky failure modes (i.e., severe and likely to happen)?
- Do you expect new dependencies to be created?
- Who will be impacted by the change?
- Will everyone benefit from the change? If not, how do you convince those who might lose something that they will eventually gain something else?
- Should you expect any difficulty in getting the target process validated by all potentially impacted parties?
- What's in it for each impacted party?
- Are the priorities set in matters of practical actions and next steps to implement the changes?
- Does everyone realize what the new process truly means?
- Has the process owner been identified, and has he validated the target process?
- Are there any side effects potentially not captured?
- Have you defined a contingency/continuity plan?

The contents of this coaching discussion will highly depend on the target process design. Therefore, the *framed discussion* is omitted.

Week 16: Preparation of the Engineer / Improve tollgate

This section assumes the target process meets sponsor and customer expectations. If not, repeat the contents of the Week 15 session.

Expect Belts-to-be to come to the session with the key deliverables from the Engineer / Improve phase: the individual changes proposed to the process, the new process design, and the estimated costs and benefits of the changes. Work with them on preparing the slides and articulating the story line. Guide them toward starting with a quick reminder of the last tollgate: the root causes (problem statements) and their individual impacts on the overall problem stated in the Define phase. Then guide them to present the suggested changes, indicating how much of the problem each of them addresses. Get them to present an assessment of the costs versus benefits and to clearly request some budget (manpower, IT, etc.) if necessary, justifying the request with the expected benefits. A concise summary of proposed changes, impacts, and costs can be presented as suggested in the section on the Engineer / Improve mind-set on page 105.

If the process flow is significantly changing, question Belt-to-be on the need to present the new flow and, potentially, the new controls suggested to mitigate process risks. Finally, encourage them to provide a synthetic summary of the practical actions to be launched next, hence ending on a tonic and pragmatic note to implement the change.

Then, analyze the challenges to expect from the stakeholders: Which questions are likely to be asked? What to answer? Can Appendices to the document help to answer difficult questions? Should any actor in the process attend the meeting to help answer some challenging questions or contribute to the credibility of the benefits? Is there any particular obstacle or stakeholder to be afraid of when implementing the change on which the sponsor should have a strong impact in the tollgate?

At the end of the session, in matters of hardware, Belts-to-be must have learned what the key objectives of an Engineer / Improve tollgate are and how to prepare the meeting.

In terms of software, they must have learned to anticipate the difficulties in convincing stakeholders to validate process changes and to clearly and transparently request sponsor support where needed.

Send the EN-E-RG-IZ-E summary before the end of the day, encouraging on what has been accomplished and recapitulating the next steps with positive actions: finalize the document to be presented in the tollgate and prepare the story line.

Typical first-level self-reflective questions related to this discussion:

- What is the objective of the meeting?
- What is expected from the audience?
- What is the agenda?
- What will be the best way to deliver a concise, focused message to convince the audience the proposed process does make a difference?
- Are customer expectations met, as defined by the CTQs objectives?
- Is the process flow drastically changed compared to the current situation?
- Do the recommendations mainly consist of improvements to the performance of specific process steps?
- What will be the best way to convince the sponsor to fund recommendations requiring specific costs?
- Have the benefits made without any additional direct cost (i.e., other than the project costs) been specifically highlighted to the stakeholders?
- How do you feel about the reactions you expect from the stakeholders?
- Is there a need for the sponsor to influence some potential opponents?

Framed Discussion

LSSC: "Hi! What's up today?"

B: "I have prepared a draft of the document to be presented in the Improve tollgate. Let's review it together."

LSSC: "Sure. Tell me more."

B: "I will start as usual with meeting objective, expectations from the audience, and agenda."

LSSC: "Great! So, what is in the agenda?"

B: "In the Improve phase, I started from the root causes, built a list of individual recommendations, and eventually designed a new process. So I was thinking of articulating the story line on this logic."

LSSC: "Sounds like a great plan. How do you intend to deliver a concise, focused message to convince the audience the proposed process does make a difference and meet customer expectations?"

B: "I was thinking of two ways: either I start with the proposed process and demonstrate it meets the CTQs objectives, or I start from the root causes and describe the recommendations made to resolve the problem, eventually bringing me to the proposed process that meets the CTQs objectives. Which one do you think is best?"

LSSC: "It depends. I like the fact that, either way, you demonstrate the impact on the CTQs; that is the fundamental message to deliver. Then, whether you start from the proposed process or from the individual recommendations depends on the recommendations made to improve the process. Are the changes impacting the process flow a great deal? In that case, I would recommend starting with the process. Or are they more a list of improvements to some specific process steps? In that case, I would recommend starting from the root causes."

B: "We have changed the process flow itself, especially for the client requests coming from North America, and standardized the flows for the different skill set teams. So, I think starting with the target process would work better in this case."

LSSC: "Perfect! So, the first message is the new proposed process flow. What's next?"

B: "Showing that the CTQs objectives are met?"

LSSC: "Yes. Take back the list of CTQs and objectives, as stated in the Define tollgate, and tick each of them as 'Achieved.' What's next?"

B: "I have a few technical enhancements that need budget. So I was thinking of requesting it here?"

LSSC: "Good. How are you going to convince the sponsor to fund them?"

B: "By showing the benefits and the return on the investment."

LSSC: "Great. What's next?"

B: "Should I list all the improvements we are proposing?"

LSSC: "Do you have a lot of recommendations? Do you think the audience will be interested in all of them? Are there at least a few good, key recommendations you might want to highlight?"

B: "Mmm…it might be good to show how many benefits are created without any extra cost?"

LSSC: "Yes, indeed. And maybe even list them before asking for the funding of the others. It will give you better support by showing how much of the gap is closed without direct extra cost, and how much more can be closed with a little bit extra. Anything else?"

B: "No, I don't think so…"

LSSC: "How about support to influence potential opponents? Do you need the sponsor to help you convince anyone of the benefits of the change?"

B: "Not really. The proposed process has been designed with the whole team; everyone agrees it will work better this way. We have answered concerns in the course of the process design."

LSSC: "Good; that is indeed the best way to overcome resistance. Absolutely avoid surprising anyone, or making anyone uncomfortable in a meeting with the sponsor. Such a situation would immediately transform the person into an opponent. What's next then, once the new process's estimated performance has been proven?"

B: "Well, I will request the validation of the sponsor to roll out the new process, at least for the pure process changes, and follow up the technical developments if he agrees to fund them."

LSSC: "Great. So, in brief, prepare the presentation as we just said: proposed process flow, CTQs achieved, improvements without any additional cost and benefits, possible improvements with additional funding and expected benefits, validation of the design, and next steps. And most importantly, as usual, prepare the story line to deliver an impactful message to the audience. It is critical to show that the objective will be met and that tangible benefits to the company will be effectively delivered."

Week 17: Implementing the change

Expect Belts-to-be to come to the session after sending the minutes of the tollgate to the stakeholders. Debrief them on the tollgate. Then work with them on preparing a test plan and a pilot process and implementing the new process, as agreed upon with the stakeholders. Question them on the difficulties to be expected when testing the changes in the process. Get them to on-board the key actors in the process to run the tests and validate the new process. Caution them about the necessity of testing the new process long enough to capture the effects of special causes of variations more or less likely to happen and stress-testing the new process even further.

Then, move to the next steps and analyze the challenges to expect: how are testing and implementation going to be practically deployed?

At the end of the session, in matters of hardware, Belts-to-be must have learned how to prepare a test plan and a pilot process and how to plan a new process implementation.

In terms of software, they must have learned the importance of testing before implementing (even for process changes without significant technical enhancements) and of on-boarding the relevant people to make the new process mistake-proof and risk-free.

Send the EN-E-RG-IZ-E summary before the end of the day, encouraging on what has been accomplished and recapitulating the next steps with positive actions: prepare a test plan, document the pilot process, and on-board the key actors in testing the changes.

Typical first-level self-reflective questions:

- What difficulties or risks are to be expected: technical, human?
- Is there a need to test process changes with a parallel run?
- How will the technical improvements be tested?
- Has a test plan been put in place, defining up front specific test cases representative of usual and special input variations? Have the acceptable outputs of each test case been defined (i.e., the criteria to pass or fail)?
- Have extreme conditions been included in the test plans?
- Is the new process flow tested as well as the individual recommendations?
- When and for how long will the new process be tested?
- Is there a need to test the process at a specific time of the day, week, month, year?
- Who will test the new process? Is everyone well prepared and informed of what to do?
- Will the tests have an impact on the team workload, potentially impacting overall performance?
- How will the people be trained on the target process?
- Has everyone been fully on-boarded on the changes to expect?
- Has everyone impacted by the change been informed why the process is changing and what value the new process ultimately creates for the customers?
- Is there any dependency on other teams or any other environmental factor to be taken into account?
- Have the criteria validating the readiness of the new process been defined?

The contents of this coaching discussion will highly depend on the target process. Therefore, the *framed discussion* is omitted.

Week 18: *Validating the benefits and transitioning to the Control phase*

Expect Belts-to-be to come to the session with a test plan, a pilot process, and a team testing / ready to test the changes. Work with them on how to verify that the changes are actually implemented as designed and how to validate the benefits of the new process.

I bet that, at this point, Belts-to-be are going to be extremely busy. Almost all the ones I have worked with have been. I have also felt extremely busy at this critical time of all the projects I worked on, but this is not because people are busier than usual. It is because it is most likely going to be easier to be busy with something else, as an excuse to work around the difficulty of changing. This is evidence that changing and validating benefits is difficult, as nothing works the first time as designed on paper. Give the warnings. *Time is not something that you find but something that you take.* If Belts-to-be do not take this time to drive and accompany the change through to the end, right up to seeing and measuring the results, pretty much all the work done up to this stage is going to be lost. Your flow of positive energy is here more critical than ever so you can convince them to put their energy toward making the change happen. Waiting too long to implement the changes and losing the momentum and enthusiasm created by the Five Why's analysis and Brainstorming meetings (facilitated in groups) is likely to have a frustrating impact: status quo, and efforts deployed in running the Lean Six Sigma initiative wasted.

So, move to the next steps with Belts-to-be, yourself well aware of this challenge, and give them the warnings. They should walk out of this session with the mission to make the change happen, and the motivation to see the benefits, transparently measured (using the same measurement approach as defined in the data collection plan in the Measure phase).

At the end of the session, in matters of hardware, Belts-to-be must have learned the importance of accompanying the change up to its implementation and measuring benefits transparently so that the new process performance can be compared to the initial situation.

In terms of software, they must have learned the difficulty of making changes happen and measuring benefits; Be prepared to face challenges to implement change, yet sit on a rocket of motivation and positive energy to avoid letting the Lean Six Sigma initiative die.

Send the EN-E-RG-IZ-E summary before the end of the day, encouraging on what has been accomplished and recapitulating the next steps with positive actions: implement and validate the new process with the team (easier written than done) and measure the benefits.

Typical first-level self-reflective questions:

- Does the new process perform as expected on paper?
- Have the benefits been validated (i.e., objectives achieved)? If not, how far from the expected target is the new process performance?
- Has the new process been measured in conditions similar enough to the Measure phase (referring to the data collection plan), allowing comparison of the initial and final process performances in full transparency and without subjectivity?
- Have all the tests run properly, as documented in the test plans?
- Has everyone been cooperative and enthusiastic with the new process?
- If not, why did people show any form of resistance?
- Have the reasons to change and expected benefits been properly explained? Have the oppositions been understood?
- Is sponsor support required to overcome resistance?

- If any variation to the intended design has come along the way, does it impact the conclusions (CTQs achieved)?
- Has any adjustment to the initial recommendations been made after running the tests? If yes, is it minor enough to be implemented without sponsor validation?
- Is there a need to go back to Measure and Analyze to resolve the problem and meet customers' expectations?
- If the new process performance meets the CTQs objectives, has it been validated over a long enough period of time to instill confidence such performance is stable?
- Is there a risk the process performance might not remain as it is?
- Have special causes of variations been seen during the tests? If yes, have they been understood? Are additional adjustments to the target process required?
- Is the new process eventually validated by all relevant parties?

The contents of this coaching discussion will highly depend on the target process performance and the nature of the benefits. Therefore, the *framed discussion* is omitted.

As an important note, do understand that implementing the change and getting the benefits recognized is likely to take several weeks. But to keep the visualization of the journey simple here, we assume it has been completed prior to the next coaching session, which marks the start of the Control phase. Yet, in practice, if more time is required, the coach can repeat the messages from weeks 17 and 18 until validation of the new process and benefits is achieved.

Control

The distinction between the past, present, and future is only a stubbornly persistent illusion.
—*Albert Einstein*

The Control mind-set

The Control phase aims at sustaining the benefits of the new process and monitoring its performance over time. For a Lean Six Sigma recognized expert, the problem is not considered "resolved" only because it has been resolved once. The new process must work in the future as it does now, forever, and somehow must become *boring* in the sense that it always meets its expected target, without any surprise. Only once the process has reached this stage can the project manager step back and hand over the necessary tools for the process owner to take full ownership of the new process. Stabilizing the changes and enabling the monitoring of the new process, is a great difference a Lean Six Sigma expert should catch in opposition to any other change leader. This step enables the process owner to constantly control that the process performs as expected on design in the long term, and enables alerts to be raised when the process comes out of control. You, the coach, have an important role to play here in cautioning Belts-to-be that the project does not end until the new process is monitored and in control. It is far too easy to get excited when seeing the new process working well once, go away claiming the benefits, and let the process fall apart one month down the road. Do not let them lose their grip before the end.

Template: the conclusions of the Control phase
Completing the Control phase should lead to filling in the following table and comments:

CTQ (from Define)	End state (project deliverable)	Achieved?	Monitoring tool
Improvement CTQ1	CTQ1 improved from X to Y	✔	Dashboard
Improvement CTQ2	...	✔	Additional Control
Improvement CTQ3	CTQ3 improved from X to Y, with remaining gap of Z	↗ Addressed in a dedicated on-going project	...
Watchdog CTQ1	...	✔	...

Overall benefits:
- ☐ Net income contribution: ...
- ☐ Cost avoidances: ...
- ☐ Risk reduction: ...

Week 19: Introduction to the Control phase; sustaining the benefits

Expect Belts-to-be to come to the session with the validation of the benefits, and, most likely, a few adjustments in the new process compared to what was presented on paper in the Engineer / Improve tollgate. Congratulate them for the achievements. They have come a long way!

Yet make it clear that the Lean Six Sigma initiative is not completed. Introduce the Control phase as the difference between a Lean Six Sigma initiative and another change management project. Make this difference looks like the cherry on the cake, the "wow!" thing, which will give a boost of Positive Energy to continue the journey up to its true end instead of claiming success too early and failing in the final wrap-up steps that will make a true and visible difference.

Once the mind-set of the Control phase is outlined, work with Belts-to-be on which tools to use to reach this dual objective (sustaining the benefits and monitoring the new process performance). Help them to build the relevant Control charts, identifying the control limits and ensuring they are well within the specified limits. Collecting data to build those charts might require a bit of time: this should be completed by Belts-to-be prior to the next coaching session.

Then, move to the next steps and analyze the expected challenges. In order for the process to be sustainable, get Belts-to-be to figure out by themselves the importance of documentation (of the new process and procedures) and training. How could people potentially do their "new" job if they are not trained to do it and if they do not have clear documentation to refer to when they are lost, or need a refresher?

At the end of the session, in matters of hardware, Belts-to-be must have learned the objectives of the Control phase, the Control charts to be used for the different types of data sets, and the importance of documentation and training in sustaining the change.

In terms of software, they must have learned the mind-set of the Control phase and how it differs compared to a non-Lean-Six-Sigma initiative in sustaining the present performance over the future.

Send the EN-E-RG-IZ-E summary before the end of the day, encouraging on what has been accomplished and recapitulating the next steps with positive actions: prepare the Control charts and measure the Control limits, prepare the new process documentation, and train the team on the new process.

Typical first-level self-reflective questions:

- What is the objective of the Control phase?
- What are the expected outcomes?
- What are the performances to expect from the new process? What are the Control limits?
- Have the control limits been measured with a data set representative of the reality, without any specific environmental factor that could skew the conclusions?
- Are the Control limits well within the specified limits, ensuring customer expectations will be consistently met?
- What is the level for each CTQ at which the process owner should be alerted that the process has drifted out of control?
- Is there a mechanism in place to ensure the process owner will be aware if the process drifts out of control?
- Will the process owner know how to react when facing such a special cause of variation?
- Can the process be considered stable over time?

The contents of these coaching discussions will highly depend on the nature of the CTQs and on the new process performance, specific to each situation. Therefore, the *framed discussion* is omitted.

Week 20: Monitor the new process's performance

Expect Belt-to-be to come to the session with the Control limits and the documentation and training plans. Work with them on the second aspect of the Control phase: monitoring the new process and handing it over to the process owner. Guide him toward preparing a Control Plan (the key metrics to be monitored, recommended frequency, and alert levels as signs the process is sliding out of control and from where the process owner should be ready to react and investigate). Question them on whether metrics and dashboards are already in place to monitor the new process or whether new indicators are required. And if yes, how practical is their implementation? Encourage them to discuss the monitoring process with the process owner, who is eventually the person who will do it: if the process owner does not buy in, does not see what is in it for him, he is unlikely to use the indicators anyway.

At the end of the session, in matters of hardware, Belts-to-be must have learned the contents of a Control plan and the importance of the process owner in monitoring the process post-project.

In terms of software, they must have learned the mind-set of Lean Six Sigma in monitoring process performance and ensuring the process performs as expected forever.

Send the EN-E-RG-IZ-E summary before the end of the day, encouraging on what has been accomplished and recapitulating the next steps with positive actions: prepare the Control plan, and validate it with the process owner.

Typical first-level self-reflective questions:

- What are the metrics required to monitor the new process? Are new metrics required?
- At what frequency should these indicators be reported and monitored?
- Is a specific new dashboard necessary?
- If yes, has the dashboard been practically implemented and taken over by the process owner?
- Does the process of producing the dashboard require efforts low enough to be worth the information it contains?
- Who should be included in the dashboard distribution list?
- Is there a need to put in place specific controls?
- Has the new process been documented?
- Does the documentation include the controls and monitoring tools?
- Has the process documentation been signed off on by the process owner?
- Have all the people involved in the process been trained?
- Does everyone know when and how to refer to the process documentation if needed?
- Has the process owner all he needs to proactively monitor the process performances?

The contents of this discussion will depend on the target process and its performance. Therefore, the *framed discussion* is omitted.

Week 21: Preparing the project closing

Expect Belts-to-be to come to the session with the key deliverables of the Control phase: Control charts, new process documentation, training plan, control plan. Work with them on preparing the Control tollgate, aiming at closing the Lean Six Sigma initiative. Guide them to start from the last message delivered in the previous tollgate (the new process and expected benefits). Help them to structure the message to be delivered in this tollgate, keeping in mind that it is the last impression that will be left of the overall project. Encourage them to highlight the benefits, *selling* the shining achievements and clearly demonstrating that the objectives have been met by recalling the CTQs from the Define phase. The template proposed in the section on the Control mind-set on page 122 can be used here. Then get them to emphasize the additional deliverables that make the process sustainable and in control as ownership is taken over by the process owner (who *must* be present in the meeting). Close by getting the sponsor to agree with closing the project and then suggesting ideas for continuous improvement.

At the end of the session, in matters of hardware, Belts-to-be must have learned how to prepare a Control tollgate and, more generally speaking, how to close a Lean Six Sigma project.

In terms of software, they must have learned the overall mind-set of the Control phase and the fact that Lean Six Sigma never ends: continuous improvement is always around the corner.

Send the EN-E-RG-IZ-E summary before the end of the day, encouraging on what has been accomplished and recapitulating the next steps with positive actions: finalize the document to be presented during the Control tollgate, and prepare the story line.

Typical first-level self-reflective questions related to this discussion:

- What is the objective of the meeting?
- What is expected from the audience?
- What is the agenda?
- What is the best way to deliver a concise, focused message to convince the stakeholders the objectives have been met and the sponsor to agree with closing the project?
- How different is the actual process from what has been proposed at the Improve Tollgate?
- What is the impact of the differences on the process performance?

- What is learned from the Control charts from a business perspective?
- Which chart(s) can help visualize the new process's performance?
- What is the best way to convince the stakeholders the new process meets the objectives and is in control and stable?
- If special causes of variations have been seen, have they been explained in the language of the business's stakeholders?
- What questions do you expect from anyone in the audience?

Framed Discussion

LSSC: "Hi! What's up today?"

B: "I have prepared a draft of the document to be presented in the Control tollgate. Let's review it together."

LSSC: "Sure. Tell me more."

B: "I will start as usual with meeting objective, expectations from the audience, and agenda."

LSSC: "Great! So, what is in the agenda?"

B: "Since the last time I met with the stakeholders, we have implemented the process and made a few adjustments to the design, validated the benefits, trained the teams on the new process, and put in place all the required tools for the process owner to take ownership: the control plan and process documentation. I am not sure at what level of detail I should present what has been done, though?"

LSSC: "Good question. Let's take the steps one by one. Starting with the implementation and adjustments to the actual process, how different is the actual process from what you had proposed at the Improve tollgate?"

B: "Not much. We have implemented all the process changes but decided to drop one of the technical enhancements, as it was too costly."

LSSC: "Alright. What is the impact on the process performance?

B: "Minor. With the new process, we answer clients within two days when the query comes from Asia or Europe but three days when it comes from North America. We needed a rerouting of the calls to have all queries answered within two days, but the cost is beyond the budget I had. Still, the queries are answered within the expected three days."

LSSC: "Alright. But if the performance you had estimated in the last tollgate is impacted, it is important to outline it to the sponsor."

B: "OK. So I will start with a brief description of the adjusted process. Then I will present the new process performances. Should I show the Control charts?"

LSSC: "What do you think? What do you learn from the Control charts, from a business perspective?"

B: "They show the Control limits and the stability of the process over the last two weeks: even though the expected performances were not met immediately, only one query has not been answered in three days in the past two weeks. It came from North America, and we found out that the manager following this client was on unexpected leave on that day. So I think showing the chart will speak: it will show the new process meets the target!"

LSSC: "Anything else to show on this first objective of providing an answer to the clients in three days?"

B: "Maybe. I have a box plot chart of the answering times per region. I think it also shows we have aligned the process performance across regions. What do you think?"

LSSC: "Very good idea! It is even a delighter as it is beyond the project objectives! How about the other CTQs?"

B: "I do not know how to deal with the number of completed missions. It will take more than six months to have a sample size big enough for me to conclude anything, but I do not want to wait that long to close this project. What should I do?"

LSSC: "Well, that is always a challenging situation. How many missions have been completed since the new process has been implemented?"

B: "A handful. Most of our missions are usually six-month contracts or longer."

LSSC: "Have these short-term missions, even though it is just a handful, been completed as committed?"

B: "Yes."

LSSC: "Alright. For the others, can you at least show that they are on track with the plans at this point of time?"

B: "Indeed, I could do that."

LSSC: "I also remember that you highlighted the steps in the process that are most critical to preventing the missions from overrunning. Which ones were they?"

B: "In the risk analysis with the FMEA you mean? Indeed, 84 percent of the risk inherent to the process laid in the answers provided to the clients: i.e., the first three days..."

LSSC: "Good. So maybe you could propose a compromise: show that the new process helps to reduce the overall process risk, and that that is proven by the missions completed and started since the new process has been implemented, and put in place the required measures to control the missions to be completed in six months or so. If some missions are not completed as planned, that is going to be another new business challenge, coming as a continuous improvement of the process just put in place."

B: "Good. That should work this way. So, after presenting the new process and the performances measured on the missions completed and started in the past four weeks, I will transition to the dashboard and the metrics in place for the process owner to monitor the process. It will naturally include the metrics related to the completed missions (within or beyond time and budget), from where I will explain what you just advised."

LSSC: "Sounds good. What's next?"

B: "Documentation and handover to the process owner: I will need the sign-off from all the skill set team leaders, but that will just be a formality, as they already run the process as it has been designed with them. And I will ask the sponsor to sign off on the project closing."

LSSC: "Fine. What questions do you expect from anyone in the audience?"

B: "Nothing I can think of. But I will check again the initial requests and voices I collected in the Define phase, so as not to overlook anything I would have forgotten since then."

LSSC: "Wise idea. So, in brief, let's start with the new process and its performances measured since it has been implemented, show how the performances will be monitored over time and how the process owner will be alerted if the process drifts out of control, ask for the sign-offs, and close the project. And most importantly, as for the other tollgates, prepare the message and the story line to catch your audience's attention and obtain what you need from them. Finally, remember this tollgate is the last impression you are going to leave of the work you did on this project: sell your work; make it shine!"

Week 22: From a one-off to a habit

The last Positive Energy PIT STOP after the Control tollgate: spend another half-hour debriefing Belts-to-be on the tollgate and the overall journey. Play back the overall Lean Six Sigma journey: what Belts (now certified!) have learned, what they would do differently in another process improvement initiative, how they are going to encourage the people around them to apply the Lean Six Sigma mind-set, what can be taken away from the Lean Six Sigma toolbox and leveraged in their daily working environment, and what has changed in their ability to resolve problems, lead change management initiatives, and drive people to work with others to improve a process.

As an encouragement to continuous improvement and to leveraging the Lean Six Sigma tools beyond a single and specific project, hand over to Belts a concise toolbox—a short list of the Lean Six

Sigma tools, together with the key objectives and hotspots of each phase. A synthetic summary in no more than a couple of pages provides a great written reference for the Green or Black Belt to rely on at any time, even without a coach dedicated to encouraging them to do so. They can go back to a more advanced workbook if they need more material to remember how and why to specifically use some of the tools, but a short, easily accessible summary will help to keep the reflex alive in the absence of a coach.

I would also recommend concluding by questioning Belts on the three tools they liked and interiorized the most and how they are going to use them in their daily working environment. Black Belts obtain their certification after running several projects, so they are likely to capture such reflex on their own. But if every Green Belt can come up with using three tools on a regular basis, without a project framework but as a simple reflex for providing a structured, robust answer to business challenges, I believe the coach has done a good job in getting the Lean Six Sigma mind-set caught. "Catch it if you can! Apply Lean Six Sigma tools when relevant!" might be the last inflow of positive energy communicated to the now-recognized Lean Six Sigma expert.

Bonus questions to ask Belts to help them step back from their specific initiative:

- How do you feel about the overall Lean Six Sigma journey?
- What did you learn from the journey?
- What would you do differently if you were running the same project?
- What do you think would work if applied to another process to be improved?
- What are the three tools you liked most?
- How are you going to apply these tools in your daily job?
- What symptoms will ring the bell to apply the tools?
- How are you going to assist the people around you in resolving their business challenges?

What if..?

When it is obvious that the goals cannot be reached, don't adjust the goals, adjust the action steps.
—*Confucius*

Now I hear you: It looks great on paper, but what if the journey does not follow the plan? What if the driver takes the wrong turn, does not follow the pace, or meets a dead end?

Of course that is more than likely to happen. The above week-by-week schedule should not be seen as a rigid structure that you pass or fail. It should only be taken as a *guiding map*, highlighting the steps for making good, safe progress. As I mentioned in the very first lines, *Lean Six Sigma: Coach Me if You Can* is a cookbook. On the first trial, you just follow the recipe blindly, and if you find it too salty or too dry, go ahead and build your own new recipe from there, matching your taste.

I have witnessed enough Lean Six Sigma initiatives successfully following this plan to assure you that it works. If you follow it, you are likely to reach the finish line. And indeed, I will be honest in cautioning you that it will not be as easy and smooth as it seems, written on these few pages. I am not saying either that this is the only way to successfully reach the finish line. I have seen successful Lean Six Sigma development journeys use other maps, the same way any journey can be accomplished under rainy or sunny weather. If you prefer the rain, go for it; simply adapt the journey to the maturity and expectations of your customers (both Belts and business stakeholders).

Regarding the speed, completing a Lean Six Sigma development journey in twenty-two weeks might seem a bit aggressive: "Week" is not to be taken as a rigid timeframe either. I used the word "week" rather than "step" to help the reader visualize the rhythm of the project. But indeed, depending on the project and stakeholders, two or three weeks might be required instead of one for some steps—especially when collecting data, designing and implementing the change, and measuring the benefits. Fair enough? Take two or three weeks if you can afford it, but move to the next "step" once the deliverables of the previous steps are comprehensive and robust. Nevertheless, if you have a challenging sponsor who demands immediate benefits, this roadmap is a well-paced suggestion for actually delivering a Lean Six Sigma initiative while building a Lean Six Sigma expert. However, in order to maintain the momentum and motivation of Belts-to-be, I would strongly recommend maintaining a weekly Positive Energy PIT STOP: further break down the "weekly" agenda suggested in this chapter, but maintain a weekly coaching momentum.

Of course, some Lean Six Sigma initiatives meet some roadblocks in the middle of the way that make their relevance and success highly challengeable. If such a roadblock comes before the end of the Analyze phase, I would suggest stopping or reorganizing the journey. What is the point of *understanding a problem* if there is no real problem? What benefit could be expected then? Step back and criticize the situation with integrity and objectivity, and answer for yourself as though you were the project manager: Would you completely stop and cancel the project? Would you prefer to agree with the stakeholders to realign the objectives and expected end state? There is no right or wrong answer, as the answers will be found in each specific environment, but Belts-to-be are unlikely to be able to either raise the right questions or provide relevant answers without the coach's guidance.

If such a roadblock comes in the Engineer / improve or Control phase, it is also up to you, as the Lean Six Sigma expert, to judge whether Belts-to-be should be recognized and certified on the back of the work completed or whether they should start all over again. Do you feel they have captured the Lean Six Sigma mind-set and key skills? Can you compensate small remaining gaps with training and minimum effort, even if it means not delivering direct benefits to the business? Is it still worth completing the development journey considering that Belts will be able to use their skill set and expertise to deliver more benefits thereafter? Again, there is no right or wrong answer outside of a specific context: discuss this with the sponsor and make your own expert decision. But in any case, following the recipe week by week or step by step will ensure knowledge and expertise are built along the way with at least something to take away at any time, even if the journey has to stop for any uncontrollable reason.

In summary, do not take this recipe as a constraint but as a tool to help pace your own successful journey, keeping in mind that "success" might have a different meaning for your customers and for someone else. It will certainly not be easy, but seeing the glass half full rather than half empty all along the way will be tremendously helpful in winning battle.

Time for a new pause with self-reflective questions for you, the coach, on the overall journey:

- Are you starting the journey with the confidence that it is going to be a positive experience for the people involved?
- Do you believe in its success yourself?
- Has the learner been properly trained?
- How are you going to practically structure and pace the journey, building each step upon the completion of the previous one on a solid ground?
- How are you going to continuously challenge the relevance and progress of the journey, both in delivering benefits and ensuring that Belts catch the Lean Six Sigma mind-set and expertise?

How long and steep the road is does not matter: in your quest to bring value to your customers, do not rest on those questions; do not lie to yourself in your answers.

CHAPTER FOUR

Objectives Met?

Strive not to be a success but rather to be of value.
—Albert Einstein

N ow that the Lean Six Sigma initiative is completed and results have been delivered to the stakeholders, let's look back at our key success factors as defined in Chapter One and evaluate whether our Lean Six Sigma journey has truly reached the finish line.

Business Impact and Technical Knowledge

Being the richest man in the cemetery doesn't matter to me. Going to bed at night saying, 'We've done something wonderful,' that's what matters to me.

—*Steve Jobs*

After the sign-off of the Control tollgate by the sponsor, coach and Belt are confident the expected business objective has been reached; tangible business impact has been made. It doesn't mean all your company's problems have been eliminated, but at least the specific business challenge gathering the interests of the stakeholders has been consensually defined, understood, and resolved. And this has been achieved via the deployment of the Lean Six Sigma methodology by Belts themselves, proving that they have acquired the technical knowledge along the journey.

Furthermore, as Belts have led the project themselves (timing deliverables and following up milestones, updating stakeholders, identifying and following up on key risks, etc.), they have learned the basic project management tools expected from a Lean Six Sigma Green Belt. Not to say that a Green Belt is an experienced Project Manager, able to independently manage any challenging large-scale program after running one Lean Six Sigma project, but that is not expected from a Green Belt anyway. A Black Belt would have led several initiatives, making such foundations more robust. All in all, the project management components have been practiced and are more than likely to have been captured as the Lean Six Sigma project ends.

First CTQ: achieved. But remember, it can only be achieved if the coach only plays a guidance role by asking the right questions at the right time, letting Belts provide the conclusive answers themselves.

Problem-Solving Skills

Older people sit down and ask, 'What is it?' but the boy asks, 'What can I do with it?'.

—*Steve Jobs*

To me, the Lean Six Sigma mind-set relating to problem solving lies in what I have called the three pillars since Chapter Two: *define the problem, understand the problem, resolve the problem*. Getting Belts to catch this mind-set is, I believe, one of the greatest accomplishments of a good Lean Six Sigma development journey. And I really mean *catching* it. Not just being able to apply it superficially when being reminded, but truly taking the initiative to approach *any* problem by refusing to start with solutions before defining the problem and finding its real root causes; truly going comprehensively and deeply to the roots; truly defining the problem by answering the three fundamental questions (What is the problem? Why is it a problem? How do I know it is a problem?); truly understanding the customer as a driver for defining the end state; truly providing solutions to the root causes of the problem rather than to its symptoms; truly assessing whether the problem has been resolved (i.e., the symptoms did disappear); and truly challenging the quality and stability of the end state, never giving up before the end.

It certainly requires gaining the ability to grasp details while not losing view of the *big picture*: a typical Lean Six Sigma expert skill, particularly developed in the course of the SIPOC and process mapping exercises where the ability to distinguish inputs, outputs, process steps, and connections in an end-to-end process and the ability to adapt the level of granularity to the ultimate objective are critical. *Catching this mind-set* also means encouraging and guiding people (with or without horizontal or vertical reporting lines) to follow and apply these three foundational pillars when facing any kind of business challenge. It morphs the learners to turn problems into opportunities.

Furthermore, if you, the coach, have consistently and systematically questioned and challenged the Belt when facing problems all along the road, *without providing any answer yourself*, I do believe this reflex of asking the right questions to understand the problem before resolving it has been caught by the Belt. This recurring pattern of asking *why* and *what if* becomes natural in the Belt's approach to resolving problems, similar to a song you hear from the alarm clock in the morning and cannot get rid of in the back of your mind for the whole day.

In summary, the Belt should have learned, over the time of the journey, to look at a problem from a different perspective (Pillar One), to ask the right questions to unveil its complexity (Pillar Two), and to *transform* it into a sustainable opportunity (Pillar Three).

As the coach, it is your role to assess whether the Belt has caught this mind-set and achieved this development objective. But if you followed the recipe step by step, I doubt it could have been missed.

Presentation, Communication, and Negotiation Skills

Great spirits have always encountered violent opposition from mediocre minds.
—Albert Einstein

Before we step into the change leadership world, let's explore the world of communication, two neighboring countries separated by only a thin border Understand *Communication* here as the ability to *impact people's minds,* eventually leading them to naturally change ways of visualizing and interiorizing problems and turning them into opportunities. Communication is obviously a critical step for anyone consciously deciding to step away from the status quo. To what extent did the Lean Six Sigma development journey contribute to building such skills?

Giordano Bruno and many other great thinkers and scientists have been burned alive for saying the Earth was not at the center of the universe; Galileo chose, to some extent, to step aside from his discoveries to stay alive. All had the same ideas to fundamentally transform the vision of the world, but the way they communicated their discoveries made a whole lot of difference. Galileo was not less convinced of his story than the others; he knew his genius would be recognized one day, when people would be ready to *hear* him instead of *fearing* him, yet he said it less strongly. He is nowadays the one remembered for the discovery. Having ideas to change the world and being passionate about them is one thing; being receptive to what people are ready to hear and do is another.

Back to our Lean Six Sigma journey: being able to articulate an impactful message that will convince people to change their vision of the process by themselves is a key success factor in the development of an expert. That does not mean revolutionizing the business environment every day; it means communicating tactfully and constructively to smoothly *drive transformation* in people's minds.

Let me illustrate what I mean here. What animal do you see below?

Now, turn the page ninety degrees counterclockwise and look again.

Did your vision of the picture change? That is the impact presentation and communication should have: speak less, but say more and get the message delivered in people's hearts.

I could have told you that you were really wrong to see a frog. You would have taken me for a fool and most likely stopped reading from there, because you were perfectly right to see a frog! I could have told you that if you were cleverer, you would see a horse. You would have probably been upset, and been perfectly right to be! When you are invited to undertake the thought process yourself, you are encouraged to see things differently, build your own mental picture, and make your own choice of how you prefer to see the actual picture. Then we *understand* one another. Only from that moment do we start communicating as human beings; we start *hearing* one another, which is the first mandatory step in challenging and overcoming our own resistances and fears.

In practice, in our process improvement journey, good communication means for the Belt to build the skills to articulate a meeting with any level of senior and middle management, adapt the speech to the right level of audience according to the maturity and mindset of the people, and impact their vision by speaking in their own language. Reaching the development target here should result in the ability to deliver a brief yet impactful message following a defined story line that speaks the language of the audience (and certainly not the Lean Six Sigma technical jargon). It requires a strong ability to gather data, as well as to digest and distil it so that it can be summarized and presented to drive decision making in the eyes of a sponsor. As a result, the Lean Six Sigma expert becomes a great negotiator, armed to become an advisor at any level in any organization and to influence top management decisions.

The preparation and facilitation of the tollgates and workshops (Value Stream Analysis, Five Why's, brainstorming, etc.) are the practical exercises that will contribute to building such skills along the journey. And if you followed the recipe step by step, again, the Belt should have caught all of this at the various occasions to do so, phase after phase.

Catching such skills definitely requires time and maturity and cannot be truly accomplished when taking shortcuts. So it is critical to build the expertise over time with each tollgate meeting and each group workshop, one after the other, improving the next thanks to the lessons learned from the previous. The Belt needs your help as a coach here! At each of these opportunities, step back, observe, and debrief. Let the Belt take the drive of the meetings, but do provide constructive feedback: you will have a lot of value in the development journey if you do it with objectivity, transparency, and professionalism.

Then it is up to you, the coach, to assess whether the Belt has caught this skill set during the journey. As for the other key success factors, answer on your own and fill in the gaps if you find it is necessary.

Change and Innovation Leadership

The foundation for peace is the understanding of others....If you want to make peace with your enemy, you have to work with your enemy. Then he becomes your partner.
—Nelson Mandela

Being able to first resolve problems by asking the right questions driven by "Why?" and "What if...?" that challenge the status quo, and second, to effectively communicate and influence people, brings us straight to the next *critical* success factor of Lean Six Sigma development: has the Belt become a *change and innovation leader*, able to overcome resistance, build consensus, and gain commitment?

Resistance is a natural human reaction when significant change is brought to the table. I would even say it is a required step before changing: If people do not react, do not resist, they are likely not to have even realized they are asked to do their job differently. They will obviously not change their habits if they do not understand they have to. Why should they? Some of them might have been working this way for ten or twenty years without any trouble. Provoking the reaction is a mandatory step: anything but indifference!

Yet changing is uncomfortable and difficult. It creates some temporary instability that is likely to be felt as a threat to personal safety. Indeed, even if change, in a Lean Six Sigma expert mind-set, naturally means "improvement," benefits can only be felt after a stabilization time likely to be temporarily worse than the status quo.

Think about any minor or major change that happened in your life recently: a re-arrangement of the products in your usual supermarket, a revised layout in your usual newspaper, a new car, a new house, a new child, etc. Did you not *fear* you were going to lose something? Behind any potential excitement, did not you *fear* the transition and adaptation would be difficult? If you did, why would it be different for anyone else?

But should transitioning and adapting systematically mean that changing is actually unsafe? Why should temporary instability be seen as a source of fear and uncertainties? What if any change process was articulated around *hearing* rather than *fearing*? What if *"Fear* the change" could become *"Hear* the change"? Try to visualize the potential of opportunities that one different letter can open.

Of course, some people are just naturally resistant to everything. Robert Kennedy himself said it: *"One-fifth of the people are against everything all the time."* Yet we are left with four-fifths who still resist, not because they carry the natural tendency to do so, but they certainly have their own good reasons to do it. People usually resist to protect themselves and their responsibilities, to protect their "stability." In

other words, because they are doing their jobs with rigor and professionalism! Only once their professional reasons are *heard*, understood, and taken into consideration can risk-free change be implemented without the *fear* to change. And maybe they are right. Change might not be good if happening the way it was initially thought from a pure design and project management point-of-view. The practical insights of the subject matter experts performing the daily process always benefit the theoretical design. Why would you be more right and accurate than anybody else who has done the job for several months or years? The Belt should bear in mind how critical it is to truly understand why the business experts resist and leverage such resistance to ensure the change is going to be safe and bring real benefits.

Furthermore, the process of overcoming resistance by *hearing* and understanding people's reasons to resist drives opponents to change by themselves: not because they are asked to change, but because, while explaining why they resist, they figure out by themselves the need to improve. It helps to turn opponents into change partners: Not only do people stop *being afraid* and stop resisting, but they start *hearing* what you suggest and contributing to building the improvement as they become part of the actors building it. Once they give an input to the target process, they are first of all unlikely to disagree with themselves. Have you ever disagreed with yourself? I bet not. Do not understand me wrongly here: I am not saying having second thoughts and changing your mind is impossible. I am saying the exact opposite: once you become actor of your own second thoughts process, you honestly challenge the current situation and truly wonder which solution is best. In other words, you proactively build your own change in your own mind, instead of consciously or unconsciously resisting a traction imposed by someone else. Then, directly infected by a flow of Positive Energy to change and innovate, you are going to become very excited and enthusiastic to change. And your stakeholders as well! The final change path eventually becomes different from the path initially expected before their resistance was met, eventually likely to be much more adapted to the whole environment as it gathers the practical day-to-day business expertise and the technical Lean Six Sigma insight. Such an inside-out combination is a sure practical design winner in any process transformation path. Yet such transformation will only happen once the opponents have felt *heard* and understood. Active listening and compassionate understanding should therefore become part of Belt's suitcase after his or her development journey, as it results in the ability for the Lean Six Sigma expert to drive the change by breaking through old assumptions inherited from historical beliefs.

Such skills should be caught by the Belt during the root causes analysis, when the Belt is expected to *understand* the problem at its roots, asking "Why?" as many times as required to truly unveil the roots and obtain consensual answers from a group of subject matter experts.

Once resistance has been understood and overcome, the Belt should also have developed the skills to build consensus and gain commitment toward changing habits by gaining the ability to facilitate working groups with a win-win mind-set.

Consensus and commitment should naturally come once the people requested to change—former opponents, now transformed into change partners—have understood and visualized what they can gain from the improvement. As Eisenhower said: *"Leadership is the art of getting someone else to do something you want done because he wants to do it."* People should first feel heard and understood and then get something positive from the change by figuring out *what's in it for them;* or at least, they must be left with the impression that their voice contributes to the decision making process, process from where something positive is going to come for them. As a Lean Six Sigma change leader, the Belt should develop a "win-win" thought process whereby the people feel *heard* and are then ready to actively *hear* what could be improved rather than being passively *afraid* of it. People become much more malleable to trade off and giving up something once they recognize they gain something else, rather than when they only feel the pain. And once they visualize the reward, they *accept*; they become more flexible to actually change their habits. Commitment and innovation naturally follow acceptance.

In other words, get the Belt to stop thinking "conflict resolution," and start thinking "win-win and consensual solution design" or "positive and constructive rethinking," eventually following Ronald Reagan's words: *"Peace is not absence of conflict; it is the ability to handle conflict by peaceful means."*

As it was outlined in the last steps of the Engineer / Improve phase of the journey, let me here emphasize once more that driving change and innovation takes a fair bit of Positive Energy and requires a great deal of optimism, passion, and enthusiasm, as innovative habits and processes will seldom work as planned on paper at the first trials. As a result, many Lean Six Sigma change leaders, realizing that improvement has no limit whatsoever, become contaminated by this passion to make things happen and just keep thriving on change. It truly is a very infectious enthusiasm. And then the flow of Positive Energy creating the momentum for success in a process improvement initiative starts to be communicated to others. Why not you, as a new Lean Six Sigma expert? Or why not the next Belt you are going to craft as a coach?

In summary, catching such a mind-set will transform the Belt into a powerful change and innovation leader, able to smoothly, softly, and professionally overcome resistance, gain acceptance, and build consensus and commitment to change and innovate.

Here again, has the Belt caught the change leadership skills of a recognized Lean Six Sigma expert and become a natural driver to change people's vision and behavior? Answer on your own, and fill in the gaps if you find it is necessary.

Time to pause again…

- Is the development journey a success, in line with the objectives set at the beginning?
- According to the maturity of the learner at the start, are you comfortable the key skills of a good Lean Six Sigma expert have been caught?
- If not, what are the remaining gaps, and what are you going to do to fill them in?
- As the coach, have you added the value your customers are expecting from you in building the Lean Six Sigma expertise and mind-set, beyond just delivering the business benefits?

Conclude the journey and give the eagerly awaited certificate only if you are confident the key success factors have been reached.

CHAPTER 5

A Mind-Set and Expertise that You Catch Forever

Excellence is not an act but a habit.
—*Aristotle*

I f you answered positively to all the previous questions and successfully completed the journey, good job! And I bet you are looking forward to the next journey. Indeed, being able to build a Lean Six Sigma expert once is a fantastic and fulfilling achievement, but it is somehow only the end of the Engineer / Improve phase. Only after repeating the exercise stabilizing the outcomes, and completing the Control phase can you trust your expertise is sustainable forever. In addition, it needs to be monitored over time to evolve in line with customer demands and remain within your own control.

How is the new expert skill set and mind-set going to be a sustainable toolkit and *savoir-faire* for the new Belt? In continuity, how are you now going to sustain and monitor your own expertise and value? Even more challenging, how are you going to encourage the many other stakeholders who walked the trail with you to become part of your pilgrims? It would be a rapidly growing snowball effect if such a momentum could be created at each Lean Six Sigma journey involving people who had one of their first contacts with the methodology, wouldn't it?

Sustaining the Toolkit and *Savoir-Faire*

Knowing is not enough; we must apply. Willing is not enough; we must do.
—Johann Wolfgang von Goethe

You now have come to the stage where a new Lean Six Sigma expert was born and is just under the euphoria of receiving his or her certificate marking the reward and recognition for the achievement. Make him or her proud but also eager to continue! A Green Belt certificate should be seen as the beginning of a longer road: the warm-up, or the driver's license—just the time when Belts are made ready and responsible for building the next steps on their own.

Such a realization can be a very appealing one: the call to continue. But here again, the coach might have to be the one who rings the bell before new Belts think of picking up the phone.

As the coach, help Belts to self-reflect once again to truly figure out what they have actually accomplished during the transformational journey—and what can be accomplished going forward. The picture of the journey can be made in two different color scales, revealing two very different images.

The first image to be revealed is made of the technical knowledge and tools: the *hardware*. Help Belts to reflect on the tools they felt transformed with as well as on how to replicate their usage beyond a pure Lean Six Sigma project. Help them to identify opportunities where and when the Lean Six Sigma toolbox can bring a lot of value to untie the knots of a business challenge. Help them to develop a few reflexes to refer back to the toolkit acquired during the journey. In action, help them to identify the three tools they would be ready to use in which specific context (directly applicable in their working and living environment) as well as to recognize the symptoms typically alerting them of when to use the tools.

The second image comes from the *software*: the mind-set and habits caught over time. Guide Belts to visualize the transformation in their mind-set to resolve problems and drive people to change. Make them understand again, as the ultimate chance before they start flying on their own wings, the power of the three pillars driving problem resolution (define, understand, resolve) and the power of positive thinking and effective communication to drive change initiatives. Even without a specific problem raised yet, encourage them to challenge obsolete and non-optimized practices, bringing them to identify and explicitly reveal hidden problems. Such an attitude eventually transforms a disciplined and very knowledgeable subject matter expert into a continuous improvement leader, looking for the better again, and again. In action, help them to identify the three habits they would take on from the journey regarding problem resolution, change and innovation leadership, and continuous improvement and how they are going to materialize those three habits in practical, day-to-day actions.

Let me emphasize here that these two images will be truly visualized and applied over time only if Belts feel their own responsibility for expanding the toolkit and *savoir-faire*, with the coach no longer giving the directions or asking the right questions to guide them toward deploying the methodology. As your legacy, Belts should go away with the means and eagerness to continue leveraging the method in their way and on their own with other people who might or might not be keen on or knowledgeable with the Lean Six Sigma approach. That is why guiding them to list these three practical tools and habits and to pragmatically apply them makes a tremendous difference when the coach goes away: the new Belts will be equipped to start flying on their own, rather than just theoretically understanding how to fly.

Leveraging While Evolving

Evolution is not a force but a process.
Not a cause but a law.

—*John Morley*

For you, as a coach, the success of one individual journey lies in the legacy and the expansion of your own skills and passion. Thanks to the value you created in the transformational process all along the journey, you have leveraged your own experience and had it replicated. You have built a new Lean Six Sigma expert, and, by spreading your Positive Energy, you have contaminated him or her with your passion and enthusiasm.

But being a process improvement expert yourself, you are well aware that a static environment does not exist. You are also well aware that success and satisfaction are only meaningful when aligned to customers' expectations. And here is where the next challenge comes for you as a coach: how can you be a successful coach not just once but forever in the eyes of your customers?

Stay tuned in to your customers. Learn from them! At the end of each journey, review it with the Belt—not only for him or her, but also for you. Receive feedback, encourage critics as a mirror for you to see how *you* look, and adapt to a constantly evolving environment. Furthermore, every journey is different, and a coach learns from every single one of them. You can walk many Lean Six Sigma journeys as a coach without being able to straightforwardly replicate the recipe, hence without guaranteeing the success of the next, just by relying on the success of the previous. However, you can leverage every single journey to make you stronger for the next.

In line with my continuous quest for visualization and practicality, let me introduce here the "Ski, Fly, Fish" model **as** a pragmatic framework to monitor, sustain, and grow your expertise, a kind of actions list to be updated at the end of every one of your process improvement journeys. In brief, Ski, Fly, Fish represents the three action items for you to take away at the end of every journey.

Ski the practices that customers expect less and less. In other words, continue doing what works, but slowly and smoothly let the inertia disappear when your customers are not interested anymore. I am not saying to suddenly stop what might still work with some customers. Simply let go to the end of the slope what customers today are not keen on seeing or hearing anymore. Abandon what is unlikely to create value for your customers tomorrow. Do not try to go back up the slope if whatever has worked in the past does not truly work anymore and is unlikely to work in the future. What was relevant in the past might not be in the present; be self-reflective and recognize your own obsolete practices, however valuable they might have been. Identify the one action or recommendation in the journey that has somehow failed or is likely to fail if replicated.

Fly the spaceships that work well now and have enough altitude to stay tuned to your customers' expectations for a while longer. Add a bit of thrust here and there if you are losing altitude and think the ground is dangerously coming close; glide when you are in a comfortable air column. In other words, understand what makes you valuable to your customers—and what the next customers are likely to still expect from you. Analyze what makes you create this value, and make sure you are challenging yourself honestly and constructively to remain in command of your own spaceship, tuned to your customers. In effect, identify the one action or recommendation that delighted your customers and is likely to be warmly welcomed by the next ones.

Fish the new trends. The subject matter experts and business sponsors you have met along the road have brought plenty of very good ideas and visions you might not have had on your own. Look for them, carry them with you in your suitcase, and feed and enrich the next journeys with these new little or big things that make a difference. Learn from the people along each journey, fish for new ideas, and replicate what you learned from them to continuously reinvent yourself. Coming up with new practices requires a lot of mental and physical effort, but it can only be made easier if you build this new thinking with and from others. Nobody can be asked to change the world on his own every day. Rather than just reflecting with your own self, identify what is different and valuable from the people around you; go and actually apply what you have learned from others, which contributes to your own input to make a difference. In action, identify the one action or recommendation you *received or learned* from your customers that helped build the success of the journey, and look to leverage it in the next.

Ski, Fly, Fish, if truly applied and fueled with your own Positive Energy, will give you, at the end of every Lean Six Sigma journey, the three or more practical actions or recommendations to make you grow with what your customers expect from you, keeping you in harmony with constantly evolving expectations, melted in the ecosystem of your customers, whilst respecting their feelings and constraints in their continuous improvement journey. The contents of these recommendations are not just coming from you but also from what you are able and receptive to learn from others. This thought-and-actions process will help you to win trust and keep it and to tremendously grow your coaching skills, a vital and universally recognized skill set of any effective leader. So, not only do you build a change leader, but you also strengthen your stakeholders' relationships and become a more effective yet soft thought leader yourself through the journey. It is a way, as Reagan said, to *"take inspiration from the past while living for the future."*

As in every change and continuous improvement journey, this is a truly difficult self-reflective and proactive intellectual effort, similar to the physical efforts required to actively ski, fly, or fish. So, in order to provide practical guidance in deploying the Ski, Fly, Fish model, let me give you a *MAP: Measure, Act, Perform.* At every moment of every journey, look around you as if you were looking at someone else or seeing yourself in the eyes of someone else, and collect your own data to *Measure* yourself. You might define a bunch of specific metrics, you might draw your own relationship process flows…whatever is relevant to your measurement. As a Lean Six Sigma expert, you know which tool to pick up according to what you need. Then, by honestly looking at the data, *Act* in line with stakeholders' reactions: should your process steps and different actions be abandoned (Ski), continued and improved (Fly), innovated and leveraged (Fish)? Decide and act for yourself. Finally, record those conclusions as a written guide that will bring you to naturally *Perform* in the upcoming journeys. Such efforts demand that you proactively challenge yourself while being patient to learn. But would you be a credible and trusted change leader if you were not open-minded, willing to change, and endorsing continuous improvement for your own evolution?

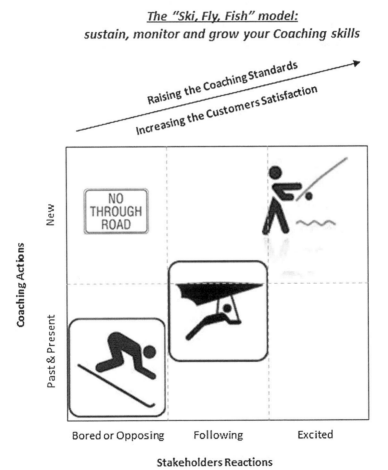

The "Ski, Fly, Fish" model:
sustain, monitor and grow your Coaching skills

A Snowball Effect

Each generation goes further than the generation preceding it because it stands on the shoulders of that generation.

—*Ronald Reagan*

The Belt and the coach are not the only two people who have lived the journey. Why not share the fruits and inheritance with the other stakeholders without whom success would never have been reached? It is true that the other stakeholders are likely to be less committed and demanding from a learning standpoint. A typical sponsor wants return on investment and direct benefits for his business and processes; a typical process owner wants his process to perform beyond any expectation; all the people directly or indirectly connected to the process want to do more and better with less risk, time, and resources. Well, pretty much everyone expects business benefits rather than learning and development. It is a fair point of view, and those people most likely got the benefits they awaited once the process improvement initiative ended. Yet beyond their own consciousness, all the people involved in the project are likely to have caught a bit of the Lean Six Sigma mind-set and expertise.

Has the Belt had to manage conflicts of interests to implement the improvement? "Change" looks like a big scary word for many people because they are afraid to be transformed and to lose something in the transformation. If the Belt managed the change well, the mind-set of those people might have changed. "Conflict resolution" might have gained a positive image and could now be called "positive and constructive rethinking" in their minds. If that is the case, make sure such a positive attitude toward improvement is engraved so that the people are becoming proactive and optimistic to change, rather than reactive and fearful. In action, encourage the teams to dialogue, hear one another, and challenge the status quo by building day-to-day discussions, dashboards, and a wide range of tools driving continuous improvement.

Little by little, people become proactive and enthusiastic to change, but very soon after the low-hanging fruits have been picked-up, the "easy" improvements have been made and the Positive Energy has run out, roadblocks come back and the status quo persists. Continue interacting with people you believe are proactive change leaders, and encourage them to further drive continuous improvements. Analyze why improving is difficult—what makes the status quo an easy yet doomed workaround. In action, go back a few months later and informally tell the key stakeholders you feel eager to change. Help them to challenge the status quo by asking "Why?" and "What if…?" and encourage them to find win-win situations when people still resist improvement even though real pain exists. If need be, encourage the start of a new Lean Six Sigma journey to define, understand, and resolve a bigger persisting problem.

In conclusion, make the toolkit and mind-set of continuous improvement become a habit, not just a one-time action. Make this habit become practical and applied, not just a nice way of thinking that remains theoretical and lacks direct application, and encourage people to take ownership of these actions, in line with the maturity, readiness, and eagerness of the people to pragmatically endorse continuous improvement.

All these little things, applied day after day, will transform the people and craft their mind-set over time. *"When you're finished changing, you're finished,"* said Benjamin Franklin. Beyond being eager to change, these methods will make you and the people around you become scared of not changing and leave all of you always expecting more and more positive outcomes when changing, inspired by what has been accomplished in front of your eyes.

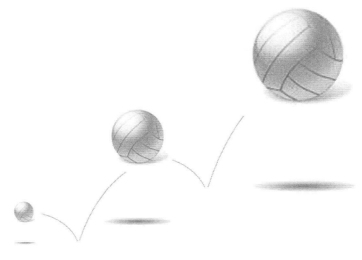

Time for our last self-reflective pause…

- Are you confident the new Green or Black Belt is going to leverage the toolkit and mind-set going forward?
- If not, is it worth coaching a little bit longer to make it happen, even remotely and less intensively?
- How are you going to self-improve and adapt your coaching techniques?
- Have you identified a bunch of potential continuous improvement leaders within the people involved?
- If yes, how are you going to help them—remotely and discretely—to leverage the Lean Six Sigma toolkit and mind-set?

Remember, there is no limit whatsoever to the world of Improvement; little additional touch points can make a big difference.

CHAPTER 6

Caught It? Use It !

*And no, we don't know where it will lead. We just know
there's something much bigger than any of us here.*
—*Steve Jobs*

aking a difference with little things requires a fair bit of
patience and perseverance, while sticking to a well-structured
methodology and standing away from easy and tempting
shortcuts. *Catching the mind-set* is your string of Ariadne in the Lean Six

Sigma labyrinth: similarly to the ball of thread Ariadne gave to Theseus for him to find his way out of the Minotaur's labyrinth, the rigorous compliance and adherence to such a mind-set will direct you down the right path, eventually guiding you in applying the method with rigor and integrity when lost in the process improvement labyrinth. So, let's summarize what I call the Lean Six Sigma mind-set—enabling real and tangible differences with day-to-day ideas and actions.

The Lean Six Sigma Coaching Process

A labyrinthine man never seeks the truth,
but only his Ariadne.
—Friedrich Nietzsche

If Lean Six Sigma Coaching could become a process, everyone would agree its performances could be improved and its variations reduced; everyone would agree it could be viewed as a systematic flow of actions and interactions: in other words, a transparent, well-designed path that needs to be followed to reach the wanted results. So, as an overall summary, let's visualize with the following SIPOC the Lean Six Sigma Coaching process bringing together the foundations and prerequisites (or inputs), the journey (or process steps), and the hard and soft results (or outputs).

The Lean Six Sigma Coaching process				
SUPPLIERS	**INPUTS**	**PROCESS**	**OUTPUTS**	**CUSTOMERS**
◉ Belt-to-be ◉ Coach ◉ All the people walking the journey with you	⇨ **Positive Energy** ⇨ Well defined **expected key success factors** (business impact and human development) ⇨ **4 cornerstones** (buy-ins and commitments; a business *problem*; a broken, risky, inefficient process; adapted objectives)	❏ **Prepare** the journey: scope a good opportunity and train the fundamentals ❏ **Structure** the journey with weekly *Positive Energy* **PIT-STOPs** ❏ **EN-E-RG-IZ-E:** dynamically and enthusiatically flow forward from a PIT-STOP to the next ❏ **Deliver** business impact, hard and soft skills ❏ **Step-back, challenge, learn** and leverage to continuously improve	⇨ A **business challenge resolved** with an improved process ⇨ LSS **Hard skills**: a toolkit to resolve problems and to improve processes ⇨ LSS **Soft kills**: a mindset to approach problems and to drive Change and Innovation ⇨ Continuously adapted Coaching techniques	◉ Belt ◉ Coach ◉ All the people walking the journey with you

Believe me: this process, if followed with patience, perseverance, and rigor, guarantees with a 95 percent confidence that the development journey will be a success. However, I have never said it is an easy process, as straightforward as walking an easy and flat track in a clear landscape. Success and rewards are a direct function of the efforts put in the journey.

So What?

Everyone here has the sense that right now is one of those moments when we are influencing the future.

—*Steve Jobs*

What is the point in being skilled and eager to improve? Why not sit in a comfortable armchair day after day, away from challenge, effort, and worry? Simply because we live in a world where "static city" is only a mental representation of something that does *not* exist! You may choose not to challenge and improve, but that does not mean staying where you are; it means being a passive victim of the future. Being skilled and eager to improve is a way to be an active, constructive contributor to your own future—a humble contributor for sure, as practical Lean Six Sigma is unlikely going to end up changing the world in one day, but still an actor and contributor. Nobody knows what the future is made of, but being skilled and able to act upon change is a tiny but tangible way to influence and build one's own comfortable perspectives.

When caught and used daily, Lean Six Sigma is more than a process improvement methodology, it is almost a philosophy. By catching its mind-set and making it practical and relevant, everyone can transform and be transformed with relatively simple and cheap recipes.

Coach or mentor of Green and Black Belts, apply these few recipes and develop more and more people who can constructively and positively act upon their own constantly changing environment.

Green or Black Belt in the middle of your journey, do not give up: when you reach the summit and see the rewarding view at the top, you will be impressed.

New Green or Black Belt successfully achieving one of your first Lean Six Sigma journeys, do not take this as a one-time effort or a checkbox on a resume: be aware of the power of the tools you have in your hands, and become responsible for applying the tools and developing a powerful mind-set around you.

Sponsor of a Lean Six Sigma journey, Manager of a new Lean Six Sigma expert, or simply a curious reader, understand the mind-set and let yourself be contaminated by the positive change thinking of it as a practical and continuous improvement method that will tremendously help you to prepare your teams and business for the future.

Yet, whoever you are, whether you consider the recipes of *Lean Six Sigma: Coach Me if You Can* relevant or not, make this book at least a guide to help you ask the right questions at the right time of your own continuous improvement journey, questions for which *you* are the only one who can provide your own relevant answers. Make this book at least a self-reflective, proactive, and practical reading on what "better" means to you and on how you are going to act to make a difference to tomorrow's landscape as if today, like every other day, were the first day of the rest of your life as a change and innovation leader.

Acknowledgments

P lato wrote that his dialogues were the direct written translation of Socrates's philosophy and mind-set. I guess writing a book, like many other achievements, is never the outcome of one person. The persons who write digest and translate what they learned from others.

I do not think I can list here all the people who inspired me in writing this book, but I would like to at least thank a few of you who *mentored* me and without whom, for sure, these pages would never have been written.

First of all, thanks to Karim, who stirred me up with Lean Six Sigma and who, as my very first Lean Six Sigma coach and mentor, made me understand the power of the difference between coaching and managing. My Green Belt journey switched on the light bulb on Lean Six Sigma as well as on the input a coach can bring.

Big thanks to Matthew for having been the one to say, "You should write a book." By continuously challenging me for the better, you made me realize that improvement has no limit whatsoever and that any incremental improvement is one step—but only one—toward a bigger goal. Lean Six Sigma and mentoring have taken on a different meaning to me and a different application for the people I am now working with.

Thanks to Azlina for making me measure and visualize what *transformation* means. A toolbox and a technical skill set is a good basis, but an interiorized new mind-set is what makes a vision really different.

Last but not least in my non exhaustive list of mentors, special thanks to Brent for being a "never-running-out" tank of Positive Energy, filling me up with passion, enthusiasm, and energy, and for making me realize that a change leader should use his skill set to always trust the future and act upon it. Continuous support and presence of a great advisor is never a well enough recognized foundation of any achievement.

Thank You, Christophe, for your day-to-day support, strength, sharpness, attuned advice, and perfectionism. Your inputs have been invaluable, both in making me a better quality leader every day and in accompanying me along the writing of this book.

I also do not want to forget *all* the Green and Black Belts I have coached and the stakeholders I have worked with: I have learned and continue to learn from every single step of every journey. You are all continuously changing and morphing my own vision.

This list does not follow any logical order of importance and for sure is not exhaustive. But without all of you, I would never have had the inspiration and the motivation to write this book.

Glossary

Baseline: overall process performance serving as the basis for measurement. The baseline represents the "topography" of the process

Belt (Green or Black): refers to the certification obtained by those who have completed a Lean Six Sigma project and proved their competency to manage process improvement projects by themselves.

Bottleneck: a process step creating a delay in the end-to-end process flow (*see also* **Constraint**)

Brainstorming: solutions generation technique consisting in quantity before quality; the objective is to get a large quantity of ideas from a group to address a problem. A brainstorming is often followed by an assessment of the impact of each proposal on resolving the problem, which aims at reducing the quantity of ideas to be implemented. Retaining only the most impactful proposals helps to optimize the implementation costs in line with the expected benefits.

Business case: the financial and non-financial benefits to be expected from the project.
Financial benefits are usually categorized into:
1) *Net income contribution:* additional income generated thanks to the improvement - e.g.: 1 million USD of additional revenues per year enabled thanks to additional capacity created in the improved process
2) *Costs avoidances:* spending avoided thanks to the improvement - e.g.: 200,000 USD per year not spent in hiring as a given

team is able to absorb a growth in demand after improving their process

3) *Cost of poor quality reduction:* wastes and other non value-added tasks not performed anymore thanks to the improvement - e.g.: 100,000 USD per year spent in value-added tasks instead of waiting and idle time (*see also* **Cost Of Poor Quality**)

Non financial benefits usually refer to risk reduction, improved customers satisfaction, improved reputation…

Capacity (*process capacity*): the volumes of inputs manageable in a process in a certain time frame. The process capacity is usually measured with a combination of two metrics: volumes and required processing time (workload, or worked hours, excluding waiting and queues).

Coaching: helping people to meet their full potential by asking the right questions to be answered by the learners themselves. Coaches should ask questions, but should not provide their own answers that would direct the learners into a pre-determined track. The learners must find the track, which will empower them to fly on their own wings once the mission with the coach is completed.

Constraint: a component external to the process flow creating a delay in the end-to-end flow, yet independent from the process itself (*see also* **Bottleneck**)

Continuous data: data that can take any value within a range: 1, 1.1, 1.112, 1.2… (*see also* **Discrete data**)

Control chart: graphical tool allowing the monitoring of the usual behavior of a process to be expected over time, and the identification of its abnormal variations

Control plan: document to be delivered at the end of the Control phase, summarizing the new process, its expected level of performance, and the responsible parties in charge of its monitoring. Such a document is the hand-over of the project manager to the person in charge of the day-to-day process, beyond any specific project.

Cost Of Poor Quality (COPQ): time (in hours, days, months…) or cost (in dollars) necessary to correct the process outputs not meeting the expected quality criteria. Tasks contributing to increase the COPQ are predominantly made of corrections, re-work and inspections. The COPQ is a good universal indicator to measure quality as it can be easily understood by anyone, with or without knowledge of the process.

Critical-To-Quality (CTQ): the few specific and measurable criteria critical to the success of the project. CTQs are usually defined in line with the customers' requirements, ensuring the target process is built to be bound to satisfy the customers. A CTQ is a metric, with a starting measurement point, and a target performance. E.g.: the number of defective cars wheels must be reduced from ten per batch of 1000, to less than one for the same batch size; the queuing time must be reduced from one hour to below fifteen minutes…

Customer: a customer of a process is one of the parties receiving at least one output of the process. Customers can be internal or external to the company in which the process is performed. A process commonly has several customers.

Cycle time: the total time required between the first input and last output of a process. Cycle time includes processing time (worked hours), waiting times, queues and backlogs.

Dashboard: a document updated periodically, providing metrics in relation to the performance of a process, at a specific time of measurement, and over the past few measurement periods

Data collection plan: a document consolidating the metrics, operational definitions, responsible parties, times, and sources of the data to be collected. Such a document provides transparency and clarity on the data to be collected before it is actually collected. (*see also* ***Operational Definition***)

Defect: a process output not meeting the quality criteria expected by the customers of the process

Defect Per Million Opportunities (DMPO): the number of defects arising in one million of opportunities. DPMO is used in the Lean Six Sigma methodology to compute the sigma level of a process when dealing with discrete data (*see also* ***Discrete data*** and ***Process capability***)

Discrete data: data set with a finite number of possible values: 1, 2, 3, 4, 5; Yes, No; Black, Green, Red, Yellow… (*see also* ***Continuous data***)

DMAEC / DMAIC: Define, Measure, Analyze, Engineer / Improve, Control – the five phases of the standard Lean Six Sigma methodology with regards to process improvement. Both Engineer and Improve are commonly used to refer to the phase where the process is actually re-designed or re-engineered.

Failure Modes Effects Analysis (FMEA): an analytical tool measuring the risk inherent to a process, by listing all the potential failure modes that can occur at each process step, and scoring their impacts, causes and ability to be detected before the failure modes impact the customer. The total score attributed to each failure mode is the multiplication of impact (severity), cause (likelihood of occurrence) and detectability scores, and is called the Risk Priority Number (RPN).

As an outcome, in the Measure and Analyze phases, an FMEA can be used to identify the riskiest and most critical steps in a process. This tool lays a three-step framework to mitigate the process risks by providing (1) a list of the causes (i.e. problems resulting in the failure modes) to be addressed, (2) a list of the impacts on the customers (if the causes cannot be addressed, the question is then how the impact on the customers could be reduced), and (3) a list of the process steps on which controls must be placed without resulting in over-processing (controls should only be added in scenarios where the causes cannot be addressed and the impacts on the customer cannot be prevented).

An FMEA can also be used to assess the risks of a re-designed process before its actual testing and implementation in the Improve phase.

And it can be used to cleverly define the control points in the Control phase, avoiding over-processing of useless checks.

FTE (Full Time Equivalent): the workload, or man-hours equivalent to one person, full-time. For example, if the contractual working hours are eight hours per day, twenty days per month, one FTE represent eight multiplied by twenty = 160 hours in a month. It can be materialized by one person full time over a month, by two persons full time over two weeks, by two persons half time over one month... FTEs should not be associated to headcounts (HC) representing the actual number of employees. HCs can only be 1, 2, 3, 4, 5... but FTEs can be any value: 1, 1.5, 1.8...

Gage R&R: a measurement system analysis tool allowing to statistically test the reproducibility and the repeatability of the collected data. Repeatable data refers to a data set that the same person can consistently collect under the same environmental conditions; reproducible data refers to a data set that can be consistently collected by several persons collecting the same type of data under the same environmental conditions.

Goal statement: the list of specific, measurable, achievable, realistic and time-bounded objectives of the project. The goal statement must be simple, transparent, focused and unambiguous. Goals are usually set in two categories: improvement objectives (what is expected to be improved in the project – e.g.: average cycle time to provide an answer to clients applying for credit cards to be reduced from seven to three days) and watchdog objectives (what should not be degraded when improving another parameter – e.g.: number of credit card applications not meeting the minimum requirements, yet accepted instead of being declined, to remain nil)

Hypothesis testing: statistical analysis aiming at making data driven decisions regarding specific assumptions made on criteria responsible for process variations. The method consists of:

1) Establishing a null hypothesis, equivalent to the status quo (e.g.: the client region is *not* a cause of process variation)
2) Translating the null hypothesis in statistical terms with data (e.g.: the average cycle time to answer clients calls across all regions is two days)
3) Testing with a statistical software (Minitab being the most commonly used), and either reject or fail to reject the null hypothesis (e.g.: rejecting the above null hypothesis would lead to the conclusion that at least one region has a different cycle time; failing to reject the above null hypothesis would lead to the conclusion that all regions have a statistically similar cycle time).
4) Concluding into the contextual terms (e.g.: the region is or is not a cause of variation in the cycle time)

Different statistical tests are used depending on the type of data tested as inputs and outputs:

Inputs \ Outputs		Discrete data	Continuous data	
			Normal & Equal Variances	Non normal
Discrete data	1 parameter	1-Proportion test	1 Sample T-test	1 Sample-Sign test
	2 parameters	2-Proportion test	2 Sample T-test	Mann Whitney
	>2 parameters	Chi-Square	ANOVA	Kruskal Wallis
Continuous data		Logistic regression	Correlation and Regression	

Kano model: a functional, visual and simple way to represent and prioritize the different types of customer needs:

- *basic needs:* what the customers expect, without even mentioning it as it is obvious to them. Failure in meeting basic needs results in dissatisfying the customers. As an example of basic needs, think about warm water in the shower: warm water is taken for granted by most people; not having warm water would result in dissatisfaction. But people will not be more satisfied when the water is warmer and warmer.
- *performance needs*: what can be improved in order to improve the customers' satisfaction. As an example, think about queuing time: the shorter, the better.
- *delighters*: what would excite the customers, by anticipation of what they would need before they think about it, beyond the voice of the customer. As an example, think about the iPhone phenomenon: before the first iPhone was produced, nobody would have expressed the need for an iPhone. Yet, so many people have become fans as soon as it has been on sale.

Over time, as customers tend to be more and more demanding, delighters tend to become performance needs, which tend to become basic needs. Illustrating this evolution with the example of the iPhone again, the first iPhone would not excite customers anymore; we are now looking at the next model: the higher the iPhone version, the better; and who knows: our children or grand-children might not even think living without an iPhone.

Key Performance Indicator (KPI): a metric allowing the measurement of the process performance, from the point of view of the outputs of the process. E.g.: volumes of transactions managed in a month; cycle time to assemble a car…

Lean Six Sigma: a process improvement and process design methodology inspired from a combination of Lean (aiming at streamlining a process and eliminating process wastes) and Six Sigma (aiming at reducing the variations in the outputs delivered to the customers). *Lean* tends to be driven by the process performance, internally, from the point of view of the process owner: the goal is to eliminate wastes; *Six Sigma* tends to be driven by the customers' expectations: the customers define what "good" looks like, the efforts should be focused on increasing the value created in the eyes of the customers.

Master Black Belt: refers to the process improvement champion, acting as a role model and mentor in Lean Six Sigma projects

Measurement System Analysis: a statistical and experimental technique aiming at stress-testing the robustness of the data collected, by measuring how much variability is due to the measurement process within the overall actual variability of the process (*see also Gage R&R*)

Operational definition: the clear, precise and practical definition of the data to be collected, and an explanation of how, when and by who the data will be collected. The objective of stating an operational definition before collecting data is to lift off any doubt in the understanding of the data to be collected, hence making the data non-challengeable and robust enough to make analysis and decisions upon it (*see also Measurement system analysis*).

Opportunity statement: a short statement of the "pain" in the process – In essence, the brief and concise answer to these few questions: What is the problem? Why is it a problem? When is the problem happening? Who is impacted by the problem? Where is the problem happing? How do I know it is a real problem? How much "pain" is incurred by the problem?

Pareto chart: a graph representing: (a) the contribution of a specific parameter to an output variable, where the different values taken by the input parameter are sorted from highest to lowest – usually a bar chart; (b) the cumulative sum of the output values for the sorted values of the input parameter – usually a line chart. Pareto charts are commonly used to identify the 20 percent of the values creating 80 percent of the problem.

As an example, the below Pareto chart represents: (a) the contribution of each process step to the overall risk inherent to the end-to-end process as a bar chart plotted on the left axis, from highest risk to lowest risk; (b) the cumulative risk of the riskiest to the less risky process steps as a line chart plotted on the right axis).

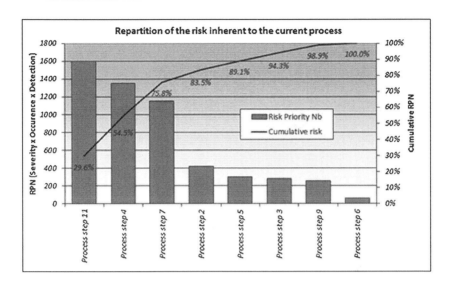

Pilot process: a trial run aiming at stress-testing in real a process designed on paper. It is a critical component of any process change, as some specific scenarios and conditions might have been over-looked even by the most careful process owners.

Poke Yoke (or Poka Yoke): Japanese word for "mistake-proofing". A Poke Yoke process is a process in which errors cannot happen, i.e. a process made independent from human and systems errors.

Positive Energy: the flow of energy the coach communicates to the mentees, making them eager to change, and even enthusiastic to overcome the biggest challenges.

Positive Energy PIT STOP: a proactive technique for the coach to structure the coaching sessions whilst letting the Belt-to-be take ownership of the outcomes. PIT STOP stands for: Positively open, Interrogate, Test, Structure, Traps, Organize, Prepare.

Process: the transformation path of inputs into outputs

Process capability: the ability of the process to meet customers' expectations. The sigma level of a process represents a measurement of its capability in the Lean Six Sigma methodology when dealing with continuous data (*see also **Continuous data** and **DPMO***)

Process map: a visual representation of a process. A process map should show the people and systems involved in the process, their actions and decisions, and the flow of interactions between the different parties.

Process owner: the person responsible for the performance of the process

Project charter: the key deliverable formalizing the start of a project, by consolidating the opportunity and benefits to be expected from the project, the project objectives (goal statement), the project scope, the project team and the project plan. The project charter is the document summarizing the project scoping stage, and outlining the purpose of a project. (*see also **Goal statement, Business case, Opportunity statement, Project plan, Project team, Project scope***)

Project plan: target end dates for each phase of the project

Project team: all the stakeholders expected to contribute to the project. The project team includes the project manager (Green or Black Belt), the project sponsor, the process owner, the coach if any, and all the people who might have an input in the project.

Project scope: delimitation of what is included in the project, and excluded from it

Project sponsor: the person providing the funds for the project (both human workforce and any other funds that might be required)

Risk Priority Number (RPN): see Failure Modes Effects Analysis (FMEA)

Root cause: *of a problem* – the components or factors of the problem explaining the symptoms of the problem. The root causes are the initial causes leading to the outputs of the process.

Root causes analysis: the decomposition of a problem into a list of simply articulated problems to be resolved in order to resolve the overall problem. The root causes analysis should also define how much of the overall problem is attributable to each root cause.

Sample: a subset of an overall population of data. A good sample must be representative of the data of the overall population, i.e. statistically having the same mean and standard deviation.

Sigma: standard deviation used as the factor to measure the process variations. The Sigma level represents the quality of a process as its proximity to customers' expectations. "Six Sigma" means that over one million of opportunities, only 3.4 defects would come out of the process, i.e. a yield of 99.9997 percent; "Four Sigma" would be the performance of a process with 6,200 defects out of one million of opportunities, i.e. a yield of 99.379 percent. When coming close to Total Quality, the percentage does not give a concrete sense of the difference whereas the Sigma level does. (*see also* **Process capability** or **DPMO**)

SIPOC (Suppliers, Inputs, Process, Outputs, Customers): a high-level process description helping to set the boundaries of the process in scope of a project

Solution selection matrix: a matrix helping to identify the best solution(s) among several solutions identified, by weighting the impact of each solution on the CTQs (Critical To Quality) and cost-benefit, hence measuring the effectiveness of solving the problem. This tool allows to select the most adapted option among solutions that cannot be concurrently implemented, and to weight the impact of each option on resolving the problem.

TAKT time: TAKT is the German word for stroke - the TAKT time is the theoretical cycle time affordable for each process input in order to meet the customers' demands. For example, in a process aiming at handling twenty credit card applications in a day of eight hours, the TAKT time to process one application is eight hours divided by twenty = twenty-four minutes. It means that if the cycle time is twenty-four minutes or below, the customers' expectations will be met.

Note that the TAKT time is a theoretical measure aiming at *visualizing* opportunities to improve a process in opposition to the constraints to be unavoidably handled. Visualizing a TAKT time target does not mean that processing one input within such a time is the *only* way to meet customers' expectations; load-balancing and parallelization can help too. For example, a credit card application could be processed in twenty-four minutes, or in forty-eight minutes provided that two people work in parallel. In both cases, the customer experience would be the same.

Tollgate: the validation meetings at the end of each phase, gathering the project team (sponsor, process owner and project manager at least) to agree with the deliverables and next steps.

Value Stream Analysis: a technique consisting in identifying and measuring where value is created in the process, in the eyes of the customers. Beyond the actual outcome of the exercise, the thought process involving the people performing the process, challenging their own practices by taking the customers' point of view, is a great tool in the preparation to overcome resistance to change.

Value added task: a task that the customers would like to pay for, as they would see tangible value in the outputs, added to the inputs.

Variation: differences between individual data collection points

Voice Of the Customer (VOC): the translation of what the customers say into requirements and specifications. The VOC is the driver to define the target end state in a Lean Six Sigma project.

Waste: activity that does not result in adding value to the outputs, in the eyes of the customers Wastes are usually broken down into eight categories: defects (resulting in rework), waiting, inventories, motion (movements of people), transportation (movements of information), over-production (producing unnecessary outputs), over-processing (doing too much), waste of opportunities (time spent on non value added activities, wasted as such time should be spent creating value to the customers)

Index

documentation, 38, 74, 123, 124,
125, 126, 128, 131
emotional intelligence, 8
Failure Modes Effects Analysis, 37,
59, 77, 83, 96, 97, 109, 110,
167, 173
Engineer: see Improve
Five Why's, 37, 96, 97, 98, 119,
141
FTE, 77, 168
goal statement, 54, 60, 168, 173
hardware, 5, 55, 63, 65, 74, 78,
81, 83, 90, 96, 98, 99, 101,
107, 109, 111, 113, 117, 119,
124, 125, 127, 150
hypothesis testing, 98, 100, 169
Improve mind-set, 105, 107, 113
Improve phase, 37, 41, 77, 97,
104, 106, 108, 111, 113, 115,
145, 149, 168
Improve tollgate, 111, 112, 113,
114, 123, 127, 128
improvement goal, 17, 41, 54
inventories, 16, 77, 79, 176
Kano model, 63, 65, 169
Lean Six Sigma mind-set, 5, 29,
31, 32, 53, 55, 69, 70, 95,
104, 131, 132, 134, 135, 138,
155, 159
Measure mind-set, 69, 78, 90
Measure phase, 37, 65, 69, 70,
73, 74, 75, 83, 89, 90, 91, 92,
94, 95, 96, 97, 100, 101, 102,
103, 104, 119, 120
Measure tollgate, 90
Measurement System Analysis, 80,
168, 171
non-value-added, 77, 78, 79, 83

operational definition, 80, 81, 166,
171
opponent, 56, 97, 98, 114, 116,
144, 145
opportunity statement, 14, 54, 57,
171, 175
Pareto chart, 82, 83, 89, 90, 94,
95, 97, 100, 171
PIT STOP, 8, 21, 22, 24, 25, 26,
27, 28, 32, 131, 134, 172
Poke Yoke, 109, 172
Positive Energy, 7, 8, 13, 18, 19,
21, 23, 26, 27, 28, 32, 35, 37,
119, 120, 123, 131, 132, 134,
144, 145, 146, 151, 153, 155,
162, 172
positive thinking, 8, 10, 105, 150
presentation, 11, 23, 25, 90, 117,
139, 141
problem solving, 10, 11, 25, 138
problem statement, 14, 99, 101,
105, 107, 113
process capability, 37, 70, 82, 83,
84, 85, 93, 172, 174
process capacity, 16, 18, 48, 100,
165
process mapping, 37, 70, 73, 79,
138
process owner, 16, 23, 24, 39, 41,
42, 44, 45, 46, 47, 48, 49, 50,
52, 57, 61, 77, 78, 98, 112,
122, 124, 125, 126, 127, 128,
130, 131, 155, 170, 172, 173,
175
process risk, 15, 18, 44, 52, 59,
84, 87, 113, 130, 167
project charter, 37, 54, 55, 57, 65,
67, 173

About the Author

A nne Ponton is a Lean Six Sigma Master Black Belt with broad experience in both Lean Six Sigma projects execution and Lean Six Sigma training and coaching. As a change and innovation architect, Anne is dedicated to transform people and processes by building knowledge and expertise, as well as leading large change programs.

Beginning her career as a consultant in credit, market and trading risks management systems implementation in various banks across the world, Anne has then evolved towards the field of process improvement. Since then, she has led numerous projects in the financial services, on a worldwide scale. Her strong skills are the results of several years of experience as a change leader and coach in several large top tier investment banks.

Your Notes

Creating the Momentum for Success

The Foundations of a Fulfilling and Successful Journey

The Journey

Objectives Met?

A Mind-Set and Expertise that You Catch Forever

Caught It? Use It !

Made in the USA
San Bernardino, CA
19 February 2014